"Matthew Parker's team of authors has created a way for Black men, young and old, to peek into a literary 'barbershop' of our own stories—honest and open, full of the pains and triumphs so very personal to us—and gain wisdom and encouragement as we continue on this journey called life, supported by our God-given community of guides and mentors."

–Dr. Tony Evans
President, The Urban Alternative
Senior Pastor, Oak Cliff Bible Fellowship

BROTHERHOOD

40 SUCCESS STORIES AND FAITH PRINCIPLES FOR BLACK MEN IN COMMUNITY

Diane Proctor Reeder & Joyce Dinkins
GENERAL EDITORS

Matthew Parker
CONSULTING EDITOR

VOICES | Our Daily Bread.

Interior design by Jody Langley

ISBN: 978-1-64070-256-1

Library of Congress Cataloging-in-Publication Data Available

Printed in the United States of America
23 24 25 26 27 28 29 30 / 8 7 6 5 4 3 2 1

CONTENTS

HOW TO USE THIS BOOK

This is not a book for the shelf. It is not a book to just read all the way through, or partly through, nod your head, and put back in the bookcase. Based on God's Word walking in shoe leather, this is a book to be used, over and over, in the business of building God's kingdom. Consider these:

DISCUSSIONS We urge you to see this as a tool for ministry. Find the stories that resonate with you, or that you think your congregation or Bible study group or protégés may identify with, and build some discussion time around them—in a group, in person-to-person interactions. Even better, allow those with whom you work, whether in a secular job or in church or parachurch ministry, to discover the stories that move them.

DRAMA Is there a story about a dramatic life turnaround that pierces your heart? Dramatize it for a group, then talk about it!

TRAINING Is there a mentoring lesson that catches your eye? Put it into practice, and show others how to do that too! Walk out those lessons and principles together, and lean on each other as you grow.

INTERGENERATIONAL WORK Maybe a father-son story moves you. Talk about it with your son, or your son in the faith. Read through it together, and see what opens up. Use it as a way to ask questions that don't have yes or no answers. You may be surprised at the result.

FORMAL GATHERINGS Read the stories together at a men's conference, and give the men an opportunity to reflect on what they identify with. It can be a Christian conference or at other men's groups—fraternities, 100 Black Men, networking meetings. Think about ways to spark conversation with these powerful stories, conversations that go beyond the latest sports scores or work complaints.

AND MORE If there are other ways that you use this book in your outreach work, please share with us @experiencevoices.

DIGGING A HOLE

Remember your leaders, who spoke the word of God to you. Consider the outcome of their way of life and imitate their faith.
HEBREWS 13:7

"I heard you both worked for Young Life." Matthew Parker's voice resonated across the table to my wife, Maria, and me as we were eating lunch. It was 1996, and we were attending the National Black Evangelical Association (NBEA) in Chicago, Illinois. We were new to the organization, attending the conference for the first time, and had not connected to anyone at this point when Matt Parker approached our table and made a statement. He went on to say jokingly, "I used to be on staff with Campus Crusade, and Crusade people don't speak to Young Life folks." My polite response was "I didn't know that." Then Matt asked me how long I had been on staff, and I told him we had been there for ten years. He sat down quietly, and our journey began.

During the course of our conversation, I learned that he held a summit for African American leaders, and the next one was coming up in the next couple of months at Wheaton College in Illinois, which I found out later was his alma mater. During the conference, Maria and I were exposed to other leaders of African descent serving both nationally and internationally. I saw Matt Parker interact with more than two hundred participants, each of whom had a relationship with him.

It was not just those public times. It was the times of personal conversation with Matt that afforded us to grow in relationship. Whether it is a leadership training event or a telephone call, Matt has the unique ability to capture and maintain the attention of others while he is pouring out volumes of truth and wisdom. I have had the chance to witness it many times for myself and with others. My first encounter with a smaller group took place soon after I gathered a cohort of leaders to participate in an executive leadership training program led by Matt. We gathered for two days once a month as we went through his curriculum. I watched all of the younger leaders in the room, including Maria and myself, hang on to every word that he said. During those training times, I never experienced a problem with anyone not wanting to come—these sessions were rich with insights and practical applications. Many, including those in my leadership group, acquired important positions in their respective fields because of their encounters with Matt Parker.

I like to call Matt Parker a visionary coaching leader. He combines his practical instruction with his tremendous influence and relationships that have been developed over his more than fifty years of ministry to not only teach but also create ministry, career, and business opportunities for those he teaches and coaches.

For the past twenty-six years, I have personally received the benefit of Matt's coaching, advice, challenges, and wisdom. This has helped me grow continually to my next level. I have also had the opportunity to watch up close how a true leader seeks input from various sources during times of challenge before making a critical decision. Over these many years, I have picked up a few "Parkerisms," as my wife and I call them. We love to hear Matt say, "Just an idea." That usually follows after a new idea or vision he is presenting. Or "On a journey," which he usually says to someone he is investing in or continually walking with in a relationship.

In addition to these phrases, Matt stated another Parkerism that helped change my life trajectory of ministry and purpose. Maria and I were traveling back from our last executive leadership training session with Matt, taking him to Newark Airport as he was returning home to Detroit. En route, while Maria ran into a store, I asked Matt if he was going to attend the National Prayer Breakfast. He paused for a second and expressed how he had young children still at home and that he limited his travel. He then paused and said something that would change my life. He said, "Besides, I'm digging a hole." He then stopped talking for a few minutes and let the words just hang in the air. Matt explained that when a colleague of his was leaving his ministry position, Matt asked him what he was going to do next. His friend responded by saying that he was "digging a hole."

Matt went on to tell me that the phrase translated into laying a foundation for his ministry and building on it. After more than fifty years of establishing networking relationships with hundreds of authors, banks, churches, colleges, conferences, foundations, health agencies, mission groups, nonprofits, trainers, and volunteers, and having touched millions of people resulting in the generation of millions of dollars of revenue from book sales, foundations, in-kind contributions, consulting, resources, materials, products, and the launching of forty faith-based initiatives—I would say that Matt Parker has successfully built on his foundation. His advice to "dig a hole" has stayed with me and informed my decisions.

Little did I know back then that in 2019 I would be seated, with my wife by my side, on a stage at Matt Parker's Global Summit held in Grand Rapids, Michigan. I was installed by Dr. Matthew Parker and the board of his organization, Institute for Black Family Development, as the next president of The Global Summit! In the evening session of the summit, I told the gathering that in a track-and-field relay event, the runner handing off the baton finishes their leg as they pass it off to the next runner to continue running. I called Parker to the front and handed him a basketball, knowing that he had played on a traveling basketball team in the early part of his ministry. As my team and I handed it to him, I told him that it symbolized him staying in the game. Since that time, we are humbly "on a journey" together as I take on the mantle of president, and Matt

MENTORING IN THE MINISTRY
Rev. Dr. Lloyd Blue

> *The third time he said to him, "Simon son of John, do you love me?" Peter was hurt because Jesus asked him the third time, "Do you love me?" He said, "Lord, you know all things; you know that I love you." Jesus said, "Feed my sheep."*
>
> *JOHN 21:17*

I was twenty-five years of age when I received my first mentoring assignment. I had been a Christian for five years, a husband for four years, and had listened to Dr. J. Vernon McGee's radio Bible study twice daily for five years. My wife and I had been members of the Solid Rock Missionary Baptist Church in Los Angeles, California, where Rev. Sydney Birdsong served as senior pastor. I was excited about being assigned as Sunday school teacher for the high school boys' class.

I had never heard the word *mentoring* at that time, but that is exactly what I had in mind for these boys. I wanted to be like a big brother, someone they could trust and confide in. I wanted more than anything to be an example of what it meant to follow Jesus.

Gradually, over the next three years, I saw my dream come true. I became their big brother and Jesus became the One who died for them, who rose from the dead and walked with them daily. They stopped thinking of Jesus as the White man's God and embraced Him as Lord of their lives. The work continued as new young men came to take the places of those who moved into college and adulthood.

Fast-forward to April of 1962, when God called me to preach and I received my license and ordination. I never dreamed that this calling would take me all over the globe.

In 1963, I was invited to preach at the church pastored by the internationally known Dr. E.V. Hill, Mount Zion Missionary Baptist Church in Los Angeles, California. My wife and I were blown away by what this church offered, in addition to the great preaching. We joined, and I got right into evangelism training. God blessed this work, and the church continued to grow.

Pastor Hill called me into his office one day, and after commending me for my evangelism efforts, he shared with me his four-in-one church strategy: the children, the youth, the young adults, and the adults. He asked me to serve as pastor for the young adults.

My next learning journey was with Dr. Bill Bright, president of Campus Crusade for Christ International and a very close friend with Dr. Hill. I spent a weekend at their location at the Arrowhead Springs Hotel in the San Bernardino Mountains.

First, I learned more in-depth about the Great Commission.

> Then Jesus came to them and said, "All authority in heaven and on earth has been given to me. Therefore go and make disciples of all nations, baptizing them in the name of the Father and of the Son and of the Holy Spirit, and teaching them to obey everything I have commanded you. And surely I am with you always, to the very end of the age." (Matthew 28:18–20)

Second, I learned more in-depth about personal evangelism.

> He said to them, "Go into all the world and preach the gospel to all creation. Whoever believes and is

baptized will be saved, but whoever does not believe will be condemned." (Mark 16:15–16)

Third, I learned that the proper name for what I was doing was *mentoring*.

And the things you have heard me say in the presence of many witnesses entrust to reliable people who will also be qualified to teach others. (2 Timothy 2:2)

Finally, I learned that to be successful at any of the above, I had to be filled—controlled and empowered—by the Holy Spirit of God and to daily walk in the Spirit.

Be very careful, then, how you live—not as unwise but as wise, making the most of every opportunity, because the days are evil. Therefore do not be foolish, but understand what the Lord's will is. Do not get drunk on wine, which leads to debauchery. Instead, be filled with the Spirit. (Ephesians 5:15–18)

I learned that I must do all things in the power of the Holy Spirit and leave the results to God.

After that weekend, I needed a working definition for *mentoring*. After much prayer and thought, I finally settled on this:

Mentoring is first listening and understanding and then caring and sharing one's time, knowledge, and life experience, based on biblical principles, in the power of the Holy Spirit and leaving the results to God.

This definition has served me well for more than sixty years in the ministry.

Now I needed a purpose statement. I began to think about all the "one another's" in the New Testament, and how "loving one another" covered them all:

> The purpose of mentoring is putting into practice the command of Jesus to love one another, by coming alongside a brother or sister and giving them a shoulder to lean on until their ankle bones are strong enough for them to stand on their own.

Now that I knew what I wanted to do, and why I should do it, it was time for me to gather more material and start a small-group study course. This motivated me to study even harder as I developed my passion and gift for mentoring. Ultimately, I developed a study course on mentoring for those skills to be transferred to the next generation. Here is that outline. It is one that has come of much effort, prayers, and tears, by the grace of God.

1. Everything begins and ends with prayer.

> This is the confidence we have in approaching God: that if we ask anything according to his will, he hears us. And if we know that he hears us—whatever we ask—we know that we have what we asked of him. (1 John 5:14–15)

These verses teach us that we can trust God to hear and answer our prayers when we pray for anything according to His will. We know that mentoring is God's will because the Bible tells us so:

> And the things you have heard me say in the presence of many witnesses entrust to reliable people who will also be qualified to teach others. (2 Timothy 2:2)

> Follow my example, as I follow the example of Christ. (1 Corinthians 11:1)

Perfume and incense bring joy to the heart, and the pleasantness of a friend springs from their heartfelt advice. (Proverbs 27:9)

The purposes of a person's heart are deep waters, but one who has insight draws them out. (Proverbs 20:5)

As iron sharpens iron, so one person sharpens another. (Proverbs 27:17)

Instruct the wise and they will be wiser still; teach the righteous and they will add to their learning. (Proverbs 9:9)

In humility value others above yourselves, not looking to your own interests but each of you to the interests of the others. (Philippians 2:3–4)

A friend loves at all times, and a brother is born for a time of adversity. (Proverbs 17:17)

Mentoring, according to the Bible, is without a doubt the will of God, and when we pray about it, we know that God hears and will answer our prayers. Therefore, ask God to prepare you and lead you to the person he would have you mentor. One of God's specialties is arranging divine appointments; you can count on it! You must keep your eyes and ears open at all times because you never know when your appointment will show up.

2. Understand the power behind mentoring.

The unfolding of your words gives light; it gives understanding to the simple. (Psalm 119:130)

We turn on the light of our mentee's understanding when we

show him or her the example of Jesus Christ by our own lifestyle. Nothing expresses this better than genuine love.

> Love must be sincere. (Romans 12:9)

Love is the will of God; therefore, to love another is to seek the will of God for them.

> Dear friends, let us love one another, for love comes from God. Everyone who loves has been born of God and knows God. (1 John 4:7)

3. Count the cost and don't quit!

> Suppose one of you wants to build a tower. Won't you first sit down and estimate the cost to see if you have enough money to complete it? (Luke 14:28)

Plan with the end in mind. Do you have the time available to make this critical commitment to another human being? When you decide you do and you make that commitment to mentor someone or a group of people, you must remain committed until your mentee becomes a mentor. I have never quit on a mentee, but I have had some quit on me, only to return months and even years later. Quitting is not an option!

> Let us not become weary in doing good, for at the proper time we will reap a harvest if we do not give up. (Galatians 6:9)

Please remember these words, "Those who fail to plan are planning to fail." Planning is an essential factor in all our lives 24-7. Most of our failures are caused by our failure to plan.

4. Take steps to begin your divine appointment.

First, you must prayerfully develop a schedule, making room for a mentoring relationship with times that work well for you and your mentee or group. If you do not schedule your time, you will waste it.

Next, you must be very attentive and listen very carefully to all your mentee is saying to you. Don't be afraid to ask your mentee to restate or explain something; it tells him or her that you are listening and earnestly desire to understand what they are communicating.

Finally, you must lead your mentee to discover the answers to his or her own questions, rather than always giving the answers. This will lead to faster growth and development.

There are three things you must ask your mentee before you close your first session:

■ Have you received eternal life, which is in Christ Jesus?

Here I am! I stand at the door and knock. If anyone hears my voice and opens the door, I will come in and eat with that person, and they with me. (Revelation 3:20)

Yet to all who did receive him, to those who believed in his name, he gave the right to become children of God. (John 1:12)

■ How do you know you have eternal life?

And this is the testimony: God has given us eternal life, and this life is in his Son. Whoever has the Son has life; whoever does not have the Son of God does not have life.

I write these things to you who believe in the name of the Son of God so that you may know that you have eternal life. (1 John 5:11–13)

■ When we as believers disobey (sin), how do we receive God's love and forgiveness?

> If we confess [repent of] our sins, he is faithful and just and will forgive us our sins and purify us from all unrighteousness. (1 John 1:9)

Make sure these three issues are properly dealt with before you continue. At the end, ask your mentee their opinion of the session, give your own opinion with words of encouragement, and establish the time and place for your next session.

5. Consider the process.

> But everything should be done in a fitting and orderly way. (1 Corinthians 14:40)

Mentoring usually works best when the mentee identifies you as the person he or she wants to learn from and initiates the relationship. However, mentoring does not always begin as we expect. There will be times when the Holy Spirit will lead you to a particular person who desires help but just doesn't know how to reach out for it. In those instances, you have to make the first step.

Over many years I have had dozens of these types of situations, and I always used the same approach. After greetings and some small talk, I would say something like, "God has laid it on my heart to pray for you and I have been doing so, but is there anything in particular in your life you would want me pray about?" The first time this happened, the brother broke out in tears and said, "I did not think you would have time for someone like me." I said to him what John wrote in John 13:34: "Brother, I have been commanded to love you as much as Christ loved me. He died for me while I was yet a sinner [Romans 5:8]. Here's my card; call and let's set up a time when we can get together."

That relationship lasted for more than thirty years.

Mentoring can also be brief—very brief. Let me illustrate. An insurance agent who was a trustee of our church was best known in the community for never being on time for an appointment. One Saturday morning he was scheduled to be at the church at 7 a.m. to drive the bus for the youth. Instead, he arrived at 7:27 a.m. with a great big smile on his face. The first words out of his mouth were "Good morning, pastor. Sorry I'm a few minutes late. I really planned to be on time." The young people were busy loading on the bus and unable to hear our conversation.

I replied, "That was your mistake. You either plan to be early or you plan to be late. Next time, plan to be early and you just might be on time. We have been praying for the past twenty minutes, so drive careful. May the Lord be gracious to all of you and bring you back safely."

About two years later he reminded me of that encounter and told me that he had not been late for an appointment since that unforgettable Saturday morning, when mentoring took place in one very short expression. He also told me that he was indebted to me for what was happening in his life, and that family, friends, and associates treated him with far more respect and appreciation.

I have never placed time limits on my mentoring relationships. I have some that I have had more than forty years and others less than two years.

6. Plan your time and prepare with the Word of God.

Make doubly sure that you plan your meeting time and topics for discussion together. This will give you time to study the topics and search the Bible to see what God has to say on them. No matter what the question is, make sure God gives the final answer. You must diligently study the Word of God until you can demonstrate that you are approved by God, aflame for excellence, and ambitious for the truth.

I am eighty-eight years of age and I have been a mentor for more than sixty years. Some of the men I mentored so very many years ago are now making sure that my wife and I do not have to live on social security alone.

> Give, and it will be given to you. A good measure, pressed down, shaken together and running over, will be poured into your lap. For with the measure you use, it will be measured to you. (Luke 6:38)

Mentoring is a modern term for "discipling." Jesus, the master discipler, mentored His disciples. It's because of what He poured into them two thousand years ago that I am writing this piece today. He never gives up on us, and we must not ever give up on one another.

> God has said, "Never will I leave you; never will I forsake you." (Hebrews 13:5)

1

CHANGE THE CULTURE
Dr. Matthew Parker

*After this I looked, and there before me was a great
multitude that no one could count, from every
nation, tribe, people and language, standing before
the throne and before the Lamb.*
REVELATION 7:9

It was the spring of 1969, my senior year at Grand Rapids School of
the Bible and Music, that the famed African American evangelist and
social justice advocate Tom Skinner spoke at chapel. After he spoke,
I made a beeline to talk to him. I was intrigued; after all, this was the
first time an African American had spoken at chapel in my three years
there. For me, it was the first time that I saw an African American
Christian man speak about his faith.

Later, I found out he would be teaching at the local Youth for
Christ, so I went to hear him there as well. I was young in my faith
and so naive that I almost literally thought that my fellow African
American student Wilma Brewer, myself, and Skinner were the only
Black Christians in the country!

Something happens when you are one of the few in a mostly
White evangelical Christian environment. You can begin to become
removed from your own people and culture. You can begin to develop
a fear of your own people and find a comfort level with these Christians whose language and biblical lingo, if you will, are so different
than what you are accustomed to. You find an ease in that culture.

Tom Skinner saw that in me and wanted to let me know that all evangelical Christians are not White! "I'm going to invite you to the National Negro Evangelical Association in Atlanta," he told me. He sent me a round-trip ticket, put me up in a motel, and even paid for my meals. Skinner had decided to replicate his evangelical zeal with its African American flavor in several young men, including me, that he and the other leaders called the "Young Turks." People like Dr. Tony Evans, founder of Oak Cliff Bible Fellowship in Dallas, Texas; Dr. Carl Ellis, who joined Skinner's staff, worked with The Navigators, and became an author with InterVarsity Press; Dr. William Pannell, who also joined Skinner's staff and is professor emeritus at Fuller Theological Seminary in Pasadena, California; and so many others.

Not one of us ever expected to become future leaders.

After that life-changing 1969 conference, Tom traveled across the country presenting a seminar for Black managers. It was designed for African American leaders of Christian organizations. Skinner and his staff understood that African Americans had a need for a different kind of operational, programmatic training. At these seminars, we learned about strategic planning, team building, and problem-solving, but through the unique lens of our African American experience.

Later, we all traveled to the National Prayer Breakfast in Washington, DC, and had an opportunity to speak honestly with each other about our personal and professional struggles. The encouragement was so valuable and helped keep all of us on track, with our feet on the ground.

Tom Skinner taught me about the Bible and about life—how the two fit together. I have modeled what he taught in the Institute for Black Family Development and The Global Summit. As a result of his rich sharing in all areas, I developed the skills to help Black Christian churches, businesses, and ministries with organizational and program development, and White organizations as well with principles related to diversity, equity, and inclusion from a uniquely Christian perspective.

"Follow me, and I will make you fishers of men" (Matthew 4:19

KJV). Tom Skinner had a group he called "The Generals." With this group, he shared his faith, his finances, and his management skills with select people that he followed for many years. Years later, with his example under my belt, I decided to do the same thing with what eventually would be fifty-seven high school students over a fifteen-year period. This version of "The Generals" started with ninth graders and followed them through college. In fact, with this group, we had nearly 100 percent who went on to college. I am proud to say that my children were part of this group as well. As adults, they are all thriving in their chosen professions—certified public accountant, physical therapist, nonprofit administrator, medical doctor, and engineer.

Tom left this earth nearly thirty years ago, but he showed a lot of men how to become "fishers of men." I am blessed to be one of them. I strive to follow his example of investment in people.

2
A MENTOR'S MARK
Rev. Arthur Jackson

Follow my example, as I follow the example of Christ.
1 CORINTHIANS 11:1

Though forty years removed from the direct influence of the pastor of my early adult years, my life still bears the marks of Bishop Daniel M. Jordan.

When I joined our church, I was an eager, impressionable eighteen-year-old lover of Jesus. How grateful and excited I was to be a part of a vibrant church of like-minded people. To say that I was impressed with my pastor is an understatement. Like him, I wanted to be a guitar-playing preacher.

How much did I emulate him? Enough to put pen to paper and write:

> Among the best of preachers; a prophet without a
>   doubt.
> Dynamic guitar player, not ashamed to sing and
>   shout.
> Truly a godly person, this we can all see.
> Truly a leader sent from God.

Diligent, careful, hardworking, Bishop Jordan was my role model, my mentor. Certainly his labors were spiritual—preaching, praying, counseling. But he also modeled what it meant to labor with his hands. I worked alongside of him in sunshine and rain—yard work, laying drainage tile, and various other duties necessary to maintain the church building. There was not a lazy bone in his body.

When I entered the army in 1968, the pastor's care didn't stop. One of my precious memories was when I would receive three-inch recording reels with guitar lessons while I was stationed in Germany.

I don't know how old Joshua was when he started to hang out with Moses, but Scripture refers to Joshua as one "who had been Moses' aide since youth" (Numbers 11:28). Joshua's proximity to Moses is likewise referenced here:

> The LORD would speak to Moses face to face, as one speaks to a friend. Then Moses would return to the camp, but his young aide Joshua son of Nun did not leave the tent. (Exodus 33:11)

The Moses-Joshua relationship was not limited to "spiritual space." When it was time for Israel to go to war, we read that Moses said to Joshua, "Choose some of our men and go out to fight the Amalekites. Tomorrow I will stand on top of the hill with the staff of God in my hands" (17:9).

When we consider these things, we are not surprised by the events recorded in Numbers 27. In view of Moses's imminent departure, he prayed.

> May the LORD, the God who gives breath to all living things, appoint someone over this community to go out and come in before them, one who will lead them out and bring them in, so the LORD's people will not be like sheep without a shepherd. (vv. 16–17)

The Lord's response?

> So the LORD said to Moses, "Take Joshua son of Nun, a man in whom is the spirit of leadership, and lay your hand on him." . . .

Moses did as the LORD commanded him. He
took Joshua and had him stand before Eleazar the
priest and the whole assembly. Then he laid his
hands on him and commissioned him, as the LORD
instructed through Moses. (vv. 18, 22–23)

Recently, scores of people gathered to celebrate my former pastor's ninetieth birthday. What a gathering it was! The mayor of the
city was on hand, as were others who had benefited from the voice,
life, and leadership of a man whose ministry spanned sixty-five years.
Though they wanted me to bring out my guitar for the celebration
like my mentor-pastor, my playing days have long been over. But
other marks of his mentoring remain.

After finishing a seminary degree thirty-five years ago, I joyfully
and humbly entered pastoral ministry and served three churches.
During those years, I was privileged to pass on life and ministry lessons to others. The once-impressionable eighteen-year-old now has
his eyes on eighty years with the desire to mentor and mark others in
ways that I have been marked by Bishop Daniel Jordan and others.
To God be the glory!

3

FOLLOW MY EXAMPLE
Rev. C. Jeffrey Wright

*Those things, which ye have both learned,
and received, and heard, and seen in me, do:
and the God of peace shall be with you.*
PHILIPPIANS 4:9 KJV

Melvin Banks Sr. was born in 1934 in Birmingham, Alabama, a place and a time when African Americans lived under the harsh reality of government-enforced racial discrimination and very limited opportunities for educational, career, or business success. Segregation in Alabama meant poor housing, schools without resources, few good jobs, and almost no ability to start a business or achieve economic success if you were Black. What was worse was that this was five years into the greatest economic downturn in American history, the Great Depression, when almost everyone was affected by an economy that resulted in joblessness, hunger, homelessness, and depressed business activity, including most White Americans.

But God used Banks to start what became one of the largest Christian education publishing companies in America, as well as to become a leader in three other ministry start-ups that continue to have significant impact on the lives of thousands: a church, a Christian camp, and a Christian nonprofit training organization that equips people to serve the community just like he did. Banks was also able to earn a master's degree and honorary doctorate degree from Wheaton College, write several books, and successfully marry and have three children, providing for his family in a way that far exceeded his humble beginnings.

This did not happen because Dr. Banks followed the example of some ruthlessly aggressive business leaders or read the latest books, blogs, or social media posts on successful entrepreneurship. God used Dr. Banks to have great impact on the spiritual lives of millions of people over the course of his life because of Banks's faithful adherence to biblical principles that anyone can apply. His success came because he actually did apply the principles and stuck with them throughout his life.

After accepting Christ as a young boy, Banks became part of a ministry that encouraged Scripture memorization. He memorized more than two-hundred Bible verses as a child, and he often quoted those verses as the wisdom that he used to guide his life. In particular, he was deeply impressed by Hosea 4:6, where the writer says, "My people are destroyed for lack of knowledge." Banks made a commitment to do what he could to further people's knowledge of God's Word. That simple commitment combined with a commitment to pray faithfully, consistently, persistently, and expectantly opened the doors to unexpected opportunities, key individuals who helped him, and all the resources he needed for the life of service that resulted.

The Word of God works in the marketplace and the business world. By faithfully pursuing the goals of God's kingdom coming on earth as it is in heaven, Melvin Banks Sr. was able to accomplish what would seem impossible for the people born at his time and in the South, the worst part of the United States to be in during the height of this country's unjust systems of government-sanctioned discrimination. God's Word committed to memory, a consistent daily prayer life, and faithful execution of God's plans that look forward to the completion of the work He wants to do through you will bring great results.

As his mentee and successor to the beloved company he founded in the basement of his home, I have received from Melvin Banks an example of this simple formula for godly success and transformative outcomes beyond what you could ever imagine.

4
DISCIPLE AMID THE NOISE
Rev. Dr. Eric Moore

Now it is required that those who have been given a trust must prove faithful.
1 CORINTHIANS 4:2

When I rededicated my life to Jesus Christ as a young single, I was discipled by an older, godly gentleman. This man taught at the local Bible college and was the lead pastor of his church. I took a continuing education course under his tutelage. I built a friendship with him during that course. After the semester ended, he invited me to his home where I met his wife and enjoyed their fellowship.

This began a season of discipleship. I was instructed informally in his home. I accompanied him on speaking engagements. I served and spoke to his congregation while under his supervision. He was influential in my decision to attend seminary.

He and his wife are with the Lord now, but I continually reflect on all that they poured into me as a young man trying to serve Jesus. I have tried to emulate this same type of discipleship when working with others.

But times have changed, and people are busier than ever. My discipleship was during a time when there were no cell phones, no internet, no social media, no plethora of television channels. My mentor did not compete with the present noise of our culture.

The challenge for me in this day of busyness is how to disciple amid the noise.

Technology is neutral. However, I used to view technology as an enemy of the discipleship process. Now, I view technology as an asset.

As a pastor I often hear people say that their spiritual life is stale. After asking a few preliminary questions, I ask the key question: Who are you mentoring or discipling? I am convinced that our spiritual life is like a river. The truth of God's Word is to flow into us and through us to others. If it is only flowing into us without an outlet, we become stagnant and stale. We were meant to disciple others.

For years I have always tried to disciple somebody. Often it is only one person. At times, it is two or three. I purposely use the latest in meeting technology to help in this process.

I am thinking of one individual who I met with once a week for two years through a virtual format. The beauty of this is it didn't require us to both be in town to connect. Our meetings would generally consist of Bible study. We worked our way through every book of the Bible. Besides me giving him input, he was able to ask me any question regarding his spiritual life.

This weekly online meeting gave structure and required commitment from both of us. This was not my only interaction with him. Because the individual attended our church, we would see each other in person on a regular basis. I allowed him to preach, teach, and lead ministries under my watch.

A few years after we ended the discipleship process, he died of cancer. I was wondering whether investing two years into his life had been worth it. Then I attended his funeral and heard the testimonies of all the people who were touched by him during the last few years of his life. I heard about his love for Jesus Christ and his love for God's Word. I heard how he loved me, his pastor, for mentoring him.

We don't always know how our mentoring helps others. In some ways I was given a gift. I had the opportunity to hear how my mentoring helped my mentee in his impact on others' lives in such a short span of time.

So, don't think of it as discipling amid the noise. Consider using the very tools of that noise—technology—to drown out all of the negative messages that militate against the gospel, and flood the technology tools with the "noise" of the message of Jesus Christ.

5
VILLAGE TALKS
Rev. Marvin Williams

Learn to do right; seek justice. Defend the oppressed.
ISAIAH 1:17

As I ambled into the house one Tuesday night, I was met with: "Dad, it happened again." Out of curiosity, I queried: "What happened again, son?" With a tinge of anger, shock, and sadness, my son said: "Two White police officers shot another Black man." Inherent in his relaying this information was a cry for a *village talk*. What should and could I say to my nineteen-year-old Black son? How should I mentor and disciple him in this moment?

The next day, a Black mother called me, asking for a village talk. Her sixteen-year-old son had seen the video of the police shooting, and he had sobbed uncontrollably. "Mom, how am I supposed to succeed in a world where I'm viewed as a disease?" A profound question. As a Black single mother, she needed a village talk.

What do we mean by *village talk*? It references the old African proverb "It takes a village to raise a child." This means when a parent was at his or her wit's end and needed help to raise their children, the entire community was invited to provide wisdom, love, and even discipline. So, for an hour and a half, I became his surrogate father. I asked myself: How should I mentor and disciple him in the limited time I have?

What village talks did I give my nineteen-year-old biological son and my newly adopted sixteen-year-old son? Though it troubled me that I needed to have these kinds of talks with my "sons," I thought it was necessary. This is what I told them:

First, you have divine worth and value. You are fearfully and wonderfully made. You are not an animal, disease, or three-fifths of a human being. God created you in His image. This means you are a partner with God and are deserving of dignity, honor, and respect. God says you are His sons, His treasure, His new creation. Your Black life matters. Therefore, walk in the confidence of what God says about you and not what others think about you.

Second, what people mean for evil, God can redeem and turn into good. God is in control and can redeem evil and bring glory from it, though we don't know all the reasons He allows these things. God has a plan for your life that will succeed. Men and women may try to stop God's plan because of the color of your skin, but God is always doing something. He is moving people and navigating circumstances to accomplish His purpose in and through your life, even through injustices. Trust Him.

Third, you are God's countermove to injustice in the world. God wants to stop all kinds of injustices in the world through His people and bring *shalom*, or peace, to every corner of the world. Therefore, you must stand up for right whenever and wherever you see wrong. You must be the ones to pierce the darkness with the light of Jesus.

Next, fight hatred with love. I know you are angry and sad and fearful. But don't allow your anger and fear to cause you to do something irrational and unwise. We will never stop injustice with more injustice. Hatred only breeds more hatred. We quell hatred and injustice with the gospel of Jesus, the righteous justice of Jesus, and the compelling love of Jesus.

Finally, this world is not heaven. Sometimes, I think we think this world is heaven. We get comfortable, and injustices shock us into the reality that we live in a messy and evil world. Incidents of racism and prejudice remind us that sin is indeed sinful. The injustices that we witness are sobering reminders that this world is not heaven. We're not home yet. One day Jesus will return and right every wrong. Until such time, we must keep preaching the good news and fighting for justice.

Though I was a biological dad to one and surrogate dad to the other, and only three years separated them, both needed the village talk. They needed someone to mentor them through this moment of fear, confusion, anger, and restlessness. In the end, I told both my "sons" what Paul told the Roman Christians:

> Never pay back evil with more evil. Do things in such a way that everyone can see you are honorable. Do all that you can to live in peace with everyone. . . .
>
> Don't let evil conquer you, but conquer evil by doing good. (Romans 12:17–18, 21 NLT)

6
TRUST THE PROCESS!
Rev. Dr. Henry Wells III

Be imitators of me, just as I also am of Christ.
1 CORINTHIANS 11:1 NASB

My entire spiritual life has been characterized by some form of discipleship. Immediately following my salvation experience while living at the Detroit Rescue Mission, God sent two men to mentor me. These two men, Al Bufkin and Joseph Williams, have remained instrumental in my life for more than thirty-six years. These men, who were best friends, worked together to mentor me and guide me through every aspect of life. God used one to nurture me and help heal my wounds and the other to be a steady source of discipline and accountability. Together, these men provided me with a well-rounded discipleship experience.

I can recall my peers challenging me about allowing other men to have so much influence on the direction of my life. One friend of mine questioned me: "You are a grown man; why do you let those men have so much say-so in your life?" I saw it differently. Although I could not fully articulate it at the time, my heart and mind were focused, much like Ruth's as she spoke to her mother-in-love, Naomi.

> But Ruth replied, "Don't urge me to leave you or
> to turn back from you. Where you go I will go, and
> where you stay I will stay. Your people will be my
> people and your God my God." (Ruth 1:16)

When Paul told the Corinthian believers to follow him as he followed Christ (see 1 Corinthians 11:1), he gave an invitation to trust God's discipleship process. Jesus gives the same invitation multiple times in the Gospels: "Follow Me, and I will make you fishers of people" (Matthew 4:19 NASB). This "Follow Me" pedagogical model is seen throughout the Scriptures as an expression of discipleship.

This form of discipleship is seen in the relationships between Naomi and Ruth, Elijah and Elisha, and Moses and Joshua. This is also how I view my relationships with Al and Joe. In every instance, the person who is being mentored spiritually has to trust that God has placed women and men in their life to guide them.

The goal in the discipleship process is not just for us to be guided but also for us to reach a level of spiritual maturity to disciple others. One of the greatest examples in the Bible is the relationship between Barnabas and Paul and then Paul and Timothy. I have greatly benefited from such relationships throughout my spiritual journey. I have been in the role of Barnabas, Paul, Timothy, and sometimes all three. We should always be in the dual positions of providing guidance and receiving guidance along the spiritual journey.

Al and Joe attended the urban studies program at William Tyndale College under the leadership of Matthew Parker. Because of Parker's mentoring relationship with Al and Joe, Parker recommended me to be admitted to William Tyndale on a probationary basis. After making the dean's list my first semester, I was taken off probation. I later had the privilege of teaching in Tyndale's youth studies program after completing my master of arts degree. Matthew Parker eventually became the third leg of my proverbial spiritual development stool.

It is comforting to know that God has placed people in our lives to guide us, people who have traveled the roads we must travel. The men and women God sent to advise me have given me the wisdom and courage to submit to God's will. They have also dreamed for me when I could not dream for myself. Our job is to trust in the people God places in our lives to mentor us. We have to trust the process!

7
HONOR THE ARCHITECT
Rev. Joseph Williams

The path of the righteous is like the morning sun, shining ever brighter till the full light of day.
PROVERBS 4:18

It was late summer in 1982. I was less than a year separated from a life of addiction and crime, a phase of my life that had spanned about thirteen years. As I was about to turn thirty years old, although I had recommitted my life to Christ almost a year earlier, my future was still quite uncertain. Between the ages of fifteen years old and twenty-eight, I had lived the fast life, the street life. Those who mentored me during those awful years only taught me how to be slick and tough, how to get away with wrongdoing. I lived off of my bankroll and usually was only one step ahead of the police.

After miraculously being delivered from addiction to heroin, alcohol, and crime, I was extremely grateful to God for the second chance He had granted me. I wanted to dedicate my life to serving Him through ministry to the least of His children. I wanted to have a wife and children, to live a life that honored God. The problem was, I did not have a clue as to how to live as a Christian man, not to mention a man in ministry.

Through God's leading, I learned about and registered for a new academic program that was being offered at my local Bible college. It was called the urban studies program at William Tyndale College. It was an innovative three-year part-time program that led to an associate's degree. The architect of the program was a man by the name of Matthew Parker. Matt was also my first instructor in the program. I desperately needed a strong male Christian role model, and this man proved to be that and more. What I really needed was a mentor—although I did not know what that meant at the time.

Every Tuesday evening, Matt would stand before our class and graciously and generously pour out knowledge and wisdom. This was my first experience taking college courses since leaving Leavenworth Prison in 1975. The image I held of myself was not good; my self-esteem was low. When I entered that program, deep inside I believed that I would fail, just like I had failed with every other endeavor I had ventured into up to that point. I had even been kicked out of the army. The only thing I had ever completed was a prison sentence. Didn't have much choice with that one! No way did I really believe that I could obtain a college degree.

Matt encouraged me and my classmates to remain confident in the venture we had begun. "Start, stay, finish" was his mantra. He brilliantly designed the program in a way that not only taught us but built our confidence and raised our self-esteem. I really needed that. He began as an administrator and instructor but gradually evolved into a mentor and friend. He stretched us in ways that challenged and changed our perceptions of ourselves. Constantly, he modeled solid Christian character before us.

Before I knew it, I was walking across the stage with my associate's degree. My self-confidence skyrocketed. *I think I could earn a bachelor's degree!* I recall hoping. We petitioned the college, and they actually extended the program to the bachelor's level, still under Matt's leadership. And, yes, I did receive my bachelor's degree and went on to obtain a master of arts in applied sociology.

I also got married to my wife, Sharon, in 1985. As I write, we have four grown children, one grandchild, and another on the way. Under Matt's continued mentorship, my ministry career blossomed in a way that I could never have imagined.

By God's grace and mercy, I have become one of the world's

8
THE AUDIENCE OF ONE
James McGee III

But Daniel resolved that he would not defile himself with the king's food, or with the wine that he drank.
DANIEL 1:8 ESV

O Nebuchadnezzar, we have no need to answer you in this matter. If this be so, our God whom we serve is able to deliver us from the burning fiery furnace, and he will deliver us out of your hand, O king. But if not, be it known to you, O king, that we will not serve your gods or worship the golden image that you have set up.
DANIEL 3:16–18 ESV

As a mentor, you are called to develop leaders. Who is a leader? Everyone! Anyone who names the name of Jesus Christ will be called to lead others in some capacity: their family as a parent, their business as an owner, their employees as a manager . . . even themselves.

Often I am asked: What is the most important trait for an emerging leader? I am hard-pressed to narrow it down to a singular trait. Often the individuals who ask this question are focused on gifts or charisma. Neither is essential to one's calling. Gifts are important to completing a task. However, God is looking for devotion that stands alone. Daniel, Hananiah, Mishael, Azariah, and Hadassah are examples of individuals who remembered who they were and whose they were. They realized that worship and service to God means having satisfaction that His audience alone is enough. Leadership isn't about oratory; it is a commitment to be God's person no matter the size of the audience. You learn the only audience that matters is God!

I am drawn to Dr. Martin Luther King Jr. as an example of resolve. Most people do not know that it was a set of extenuating circumstances that pushed him into leadership during the Montgomery Bus Boycott. He was a young pastor with a young wife and newborn daughter, and on his first assignment. He was chosen to lead the Montgomery Improvement Association, not because of his gifts but out of convenience to the other Black pastors. He was new in town. It's believed that the other pastors did not want to sacrifice their relationships and ultimately their safety.

In the early days of the boycott, Dr. King was overwhelmed with the anxiety of the moment. He records this tense moment in his book *Stride toward Freedom: The Montgomery Story*.

> I was ready to give up. . . . In this state of exhaustion, when my courage had all but gone, I decided to take my problem to God. With my head in my hands, I bowed over the kitchen table and prayed aloud. . . .
>
> At that moment I experienced the presence of the Divine as I had never experienced Him before. It seemed as though I could hear the quiet assurance of an inner voice saying: "Stand up for righteousness, stand up for truth; and God will be at your side forever." Almost at once my fears began to go. My uncertainty disappeared. I was ready to face anything.*

Leaders with resolve are not without fear. It is just the opposite. Leaders are weighed down in fear! However, they are buoyed by resolve, and leaders who name the name of Jesus Christ have a singular dedication to Him that fuels their courage.

As mentors, we must help people see that a commitment to resolve is not a singular event. It is repeated throughout our journey.

---

* Martin Luther King Jr., *Stride toward Freedom: The Montgomery Story* (New York: Ballantine Books, 1960), 108–9. First published 1958.

January was the month Dr. King normally set aside for vacation and refreshment. In 1967, James Bevel traveled to Jamaica to meet with Dr. King. He planted a seed in Dr. King to review United States involvement in Vietnam, begun during the Eisenhower presidency and escalated under President Kennedy. In 1967, the war was under the watch of another president, Lyndon B. Johnson. Dr. King began to study the war in Vietnam.

April 4, 1967, just one year before he was assassinated, Dr. King gave a speech on the Vietnam War at the famous Riverside Church in New York City. The criticism against Dr. King was significant. Civil rights leaders stood against him publicly. The president of the United States, Lyndon B. Johnson, revoked his open invitation for Dr. King to speak with him. Dr. King had cemented his commitment to confront three evils: racism, poverty, and war. It is said that this multilevel commitment may have hastened his assassination.

The disciple Peter had resolve, too (Matthew 14:22–33). Jesus was walking on water in the middle of the night; Scripture says it was during the fourth watch of night (between 3 a.m. and 6 a.m.). While walking past His disciples, Jesus noticed His disciples going in the same direction in a boat. Peter made a request to Jesus, saying that if it were Jesus, "Command me to come to you" (v. 28 ESV). Jesus said, "Come!" Peter stepped out of the boat and walked toward Jesus. The remaining disciples observed this from within the boat. Scripture says that "when he saw the wind, he was afraid" (v. 30). Yet, when he focused on the audience of One—Jesus—Peter was able to summon the courage to walk on water!

Beloved, when Jesus bids us "Come" in His service, we will face all kinds of distractions: winds, insults, criticism, isolation, fear, anxiety, aloneness, and death. We must remember it is the audience of Jesus that keeps us company and allows us to do His will.

Courage. Not looking over one's shoulder, not to what other people might think or do—but looking to an audience of One.

9
BLOOM WHERE YOU ARE PLANTED
Dr. Michael R. Lyles

But he said to me, "My grace is sufficient for you, for my power is made perfect in weakness." Therefore I will boast all the more gladly about my weaknesses, so that Christ's power may rest on me. That is why, for Christ's sake, I delight in weaknesses, in insults, in hardships, in persecutions, in difficulties. For when I am weak, then I am strong.
2 CORINTHIANS 12:9–10

Most students know that having a great teacher makes a class a lot easier. During my medical training, Dr. David Larson had the reputation of being a great teacher and a dedicated Christian. I longed to have him as a professor and took a class in prison psychiatry just to work with him. The class was every Wednesday for a full day at a prison thirty miles away from our campus. I got hopelessly lost on my first trip there, so Dr. Larson offered for me to ride with him to and from the prison. I was not aware that the real teaching would occur not in the prison but during the commute.

We spent two hours together on this round-trip commute every Wednesday for a year. We discussed the clinical situations of the prisoners that we were treating but also much more. He wanted to know how I was thinking and why I was thinking the way that I did about the treatment of each prisoner. I quickly began to rack up many mistakes and became painfully aware of what I did not know. Dr. Larson sensed my frustration and praised me for owning my mistakes and being honest about them.

He encouraged me to "bloom where you are planted." In other words, honestly own where you are "planted" and look to improve from there. Blooming does not make excuses or blame others. It is not accomplished by listening to others who assume that you cannot grow and get better. It is not limiting yourself because of your background, financial status, self-doubt, or lack of popularity. It is not focusing on what you cannot do well but instead learning from that. It is a determined focus on working the process to grow and bloom where you are, until you are planted somewhere else.

This man that I idolized talked openly, having had his own doubts and fears about being good enough to go to medical school as a blue-collar guy attending a school with students from wealthy backgrounds. He spoke of how he struggled to learn how to do research and how he had to seek God in desperate prayer often to survive the stress of the learning process. He viewed himself as a struggling professor who was still learning his job. He was trying to bloom for Jesus while planted in a place of self-doubt and struggle. He encouraged me to celebrate my failures and weaknesses because they would force me toward God-enabled learning and growth. He said that this process would always end well. I was horrified and encouraged at the same time by his transparency and self-disclosure!

Dr. Larson's honesty was one of the greatest gifts anyone has ever given to me.

In the years that followed, he became very esteemed as a researcher and global teacher. The American Psychiatric Association awarded him the Oskar Pfister Award for excellence in research on the relationship between religion and mental health. This from a man who was openly planted in a place of self-doubt and struggle. I remember his exhortation to work the educational process diligently, as "to the Lord, and not unto men" (Colossians 3:23 KJV), and to leave the outcome to God. Bloom by trusting God every day—through the good days and the hard ones that we are planted in. Trust God to be in control of the process and don't worry about the outcome. "Bloom where you are planted" helped me through many life challenges and a demanding career that has made human trauma and stress my daily experience.

Work the process faithfully, leaving the outcome in God's hands. Bloom where you are planted by God, give thanks for where you are planted by God, and the outcome will be God-directed (see Romans 8:28).

I learned three things about mentorship from Dave. First, we spent time together—a lot of time—and we got to know and trust each other. Second, he was honest and transparent about his struggles instead of putting up a false front. His modeling of strength in weakness magnified how God works in the lives of ordinary, flawed people—like me (see 2 Corinthians 4:7). He modeled the celebration of weakness in the pursuit of the power of God. Third, he directed me to the ultimate mentor, Jesus, and encouraged me to learn of His ways, not just Dave's. As Dave would quote, "In every thing give thanks [even in weaknesses and struggles]: for this is the will of God in Christ Jesus concerning you" (1 Thessalonians 5:18 KJV). For when we are weak (own it), we are strong by using God's strength in adversity (see 2 Corinthians 12:9–10).

Dave died in his early fifties, but his willingness to give the gifts of time and honesty lives on in my life and the lives of those that I am blessed to mentor.

10
UNDERSTAND THE TIMES
Dr. Lee N. June

There is a time for everything, and a season for every activity under the heavens.
ECCLESIASTES 3:1

Early in life, I had great mentors and heard them use phrases such as "We stand on the shoulders of giants," "We must give back," and "The world did not begin with you." As I mentor, I try to keep those sayings in mind and then pass them on to future generations.

I try to embed in those I mentor, particularly Black students, that they must be prepared for the opportunities that will come their way. I challenge them to be ready to seize the opportunity when it comes. God prepares us for our future roles, even when we are unaware this is occurring. God then uses our experiences as tools for tasks ahead. Our experiences are often our training ground.

As a young person, Moses lived in a palace where he learned important skills and gained knowledge about Pharaoh. This experience served him well when God later called him into service. Likewise, David's experience as a shepherd was useful when he became king. David moved from shepherding a flock of sheep to shepherding a nation of people.

There is a task in God's kingdom for everyone. Therefore, we need to first understand what God's specific plan for us is. We also need to be cognizant of the time and season of life, and what place God has for us in that season. While walking in God's plan for our life, we mentor the next generation to help them discover what God is planning and uniquely qualifying them to do.

Why is it so important to help mentees realize that we stand on the shoulders of others and that our time on earth is important but only for a season? When we fail to realize this and do not impart this to mentees, we can get a big head and begin to think that "everything revolves around me." We can exaggerate our importance and fail to remember that our time on earth is limited and circumscribed.

> For by the grace given me I say to every one of you: Do not think of yourself more highly than you ought, but rather think of yourself with sober judgment, in accordance with the faith God has distributed to each of you. (Romans 12:3)

Two biblical examples immediately come to mind about individuals who forgot this. In each case, it led to devastating outcomes. Consider the case of King Nebuchadnezzar (Daniel 4:28–33) and the parable of the certain man that God called a "fool" (Luke 12:13–21). Nebuchadnezzar thought that he was the man, that all the grandeur that he was experiencing was because of him. In the case of the "fool," as Jesus described him, he failed to realize that what he had acquired was because of God. He began to make presumptuous plans and assumed he was going to live a long time.

As one who has spent much time in higher education, mentoring has brought me extraordinary joy. It is so rewarding to witness young people come to college as first-year students, become leaders on campus, graduate, and go and become justice fighters and change agents for good.

We are important in God's eyes. Jesus came that we might have life and have it more abundantly (see John 10:10), but this promise is given in view of us living in His will and according to His purpose. We want to make sure that when we mentor someone, we keep purpose and understanding the times in view, and that humility is the fruit of that thinking.

MENTOR WITH HUMILITY

Rev. Dr. Noel Hutchinson

For by the grace given me I say to every one of you:
Do not think of yourself more highly than you ought,
but rather think of yourself with sober judgment,
in accordance with the faith God has distributed to
each of you. For just as each of us has one body with
many members, and these members do not all have the
same function, so in Christ we, though many, form
one body, and each member belongs to all the others.
We have different gifts, according to the grace given
to each of us. If your gift is prophesying, then prophesy
in accordance with your faith; if it is serving, then
serve; if it is teaching, then teach; if it is to encourage,
then give encouragement; if it is giving, then give
generously; if it is to lead, do it diligently;
if it is to show mercy, do it cheerfully.
ROMANS 12:3–8

"You need to talk to Dr. Taylor." The year was 1994. By now, I was fully immersed as a "Concorder"—someone who is part of the family of the Concord Baptist Church in Brooklyn, New York. The love between its people and me, ongoing to this day, had been cemented. In the midst of this I was wrestling with a major issue. I was speaking to the building engineer, with whom I'd developed a friendship. He suggested that I talk to Dr. Taylor about it.

Dr. Gardner Calvin Taylor was known as "the dean of American preaching" and perhaps the greatest preacher of the past one hundred years. He was the son of a Baptist preacher and the grandson of slaves, a confidante to Dr. Martin Luther King Jr., an active supporter of the Civil Rights Movement, one of the fathers of the Progressive National Baptist Convention, and the senior pastor of Concord for forty-two years.

Many, rightfully so, focus on the preaching gift that was Dr. Taylor's. He married keen intellect, passion, an awareness of culture, and the African American pathos, mixing them with the great truths of the Bible, achieving powerful results. It is safe to say that there will never be another voice like his. What is not as often mentioned is his approach to ministry. Dr. Taylor purposely steered his labor away from sensationalism and toward excellence. He maintained a regal bearing, but with the common touch, and his dress was business-like—an understated elegance—because of the seriousness, for him, of the gospel. That approach spread to the membership; many a Concorder talks about being "Taylor made."

During my time at Concord, Dr. Taylor was in the midst of compiling the six-volume set *The Words of Gardner Taylor* with Dr. Edward Taylor. He also gave the inauguration sermon for President Bill Clinton and was instrumental in having the late Nelson Mandela, the historical figure who transformed South Africa's apartheid structure with his activism and ultimately as its first Black president, speak at the Concord Church. All of these things were mind-boggling—then and now—but my fondest memories of him have much more to do with his personhood than his preaching.

When I went to see Dr. Taylor, he was pastor emeritus and maintained an office in the building across the street from the church. Once a year Dr. Gary Simpson, the current pastor, would have himself, Dr. Taylor, me, and Rev. Charles Gill, the other staff pastor, have dinner, where we would discuss a variety of subjects. Periodically, Dr. Taylor would need assistance with various things for his office, and I would work with him and his secretary.

But talking to him about myself was different. Although he was cordial in our every interaction, I was still nervous. I called him and I met him at his office. After explaining my situation, I remember him praying for me—*me*—at one of the lowest periods of my life. This began a connection that remained until his death. He recommended me, with two others, to a church in Memphis, where I became the pastor. The last time I saw him, I was in his home with a Memphis colleague and shared homemade peanut brittle courtesy of Dr. Edward Taylor.

I also remember him at the graveside of a former deacon—one of his friends—and when it was time to do the committal, I looked at him, out of respect, and he looked at me, nodded, and bowed his head with the rest of those gathered, signaling for me to proceed. I remember some of our conversations and the way he could give stern advice, seasoned with grace, as he also built you up with his kind words of encouragement.

What should we take away from this life well lived? I watched the love he had for people and fellow clergy, and I remember his humility. He was one who had the presidents of nations as personal friends yet remembered and fellowshipped with the regular salt-of-the-earth people. In addition, he was one who through his ministry always attempted to totally honor and be yielded to Jesus Christ. In a day when many of us with far less credentials put on airs, we would do well to focus on that which is most important. The passage in the book of Romans at the beginning of this reading makes an emphasis of putting our worth in perspective, as we are a part of the larger witness of the church. As walking billboards for God, may our witness so shine that when people give us accolades, they point through and past us to God.

12

POWER OF PARALLEL EXPERIENCES

Rev. Terry Robinson

A student is not above the teacher; but everyone, when he has been fully trained, will be like his teacher.
LUKE 6:40 NASB

It was the summer of 1978. My mentee, Randy Stevenson, had just returned from a ten-week summer mission project serving in the inner city of Chicago. He had lived and served alongside twenty other college students from early June through the first week in August. When I met him back on campus at Louisiana Tech University, he was a transformed man. I could see where he had grown in the character and competencies of Christ. Also, I could see the same changes in him that had occurred in me when I went on the Chicago Summer Project three years prior. Randy would go back two more additional summers and invite two of his mentees to serve on the project as well.

Years later as I reflect on that time, I see a principle of exposing those whom God has entrusted to us in the environment and culture that helped shape us. It was on that short-term summer mission project that I learned how to have meaningful devotions, how to study God's Word, how to share my faith, how to pray, how to defend the faith through apologetics, and how to serve, love, and care for the marginalized and the least of these. I saw the same things taking shape in Randy's life.

It was significant for Randy to have the same experience I had. It gave us something in common around which we could fellowship, something both of us could relate to. I could tell him about ministering to those who did not have much, who may not be in church, who may not understand a lot about spiritual things . . . but there was nothing like having him experience these things firsthand. Now we had something substantial we could talk about! He could come back and ask me questions that were not just theoretical but practical and based on his own lived experience. I could share with him something concrete, having had the same experience three years beforehand.

Since that time, Randy went on to apply this principle in his mentorship by involving his mentees in the Chicago Summer Project. He eventually founded and now serves as lead pastor of a church in New Orleans. All of his mentees now serve either as pastors or elders! He speaks often of those life-changing experiences on the Chicago Summer Project. I am so very encouraged to see the fruit of our shared experience.

In the ministry of Cru at which I have had the opportunity to serve for more than forty-three years, this principle rings out. "One of the most significant things any leader can do is to get disciples immersed in as many growth-enhancing experiences as possible. In these experiences disciples take steps of faith, minister to others, and benefit from Christian communities."*

Jesus places an emphasis on being "fully trained." Knowledge alone is not enough in mentoring, but we need to immerse, expose, and involve our pupils in experiences that have proved meaningful to the mentor. This can be a powerful tool in helping those we mentor to grow exponentially. This is an important ingredient in being "fully trained."

Take some time today to reflect on the experiences that were building blocks in your personal life and zero in on one or two that

* "How to Use Collaborative Discipleship," Cru, accessed April 27, 2023, https://www.cru.org/us/en/train-and-grow/help-others-grow/collaborative-discipleship/lessons/4c-how-to-use-collaborative-discipleship.html.

13
MUTUALITY IN MENTORING
Karl Bell

Owe nothing to any one except mutual love.
ROMANS 13:8 WNT

For more than thirty years I had one of the best relationships—with an extremely successful Black entrepreneur and philanthropist. We were first introduced through a mutual relationship at the church we attended. I then found out that he was a customer at the bank where I worked. He stayed in touch regularly. I eventually took a position at another bank, and he became a customer once again. That was when our relationship truly blossomed. As I serviced his account, he provided me career advice and cultural exposure. Eventually our paths would separate as my career evolved and his banking needs expanded as his territory enlarged. He was a mentor of sorts, paying attention to what I was doing and following me, albeit from afar.

For more than twenty years, my friend would find a reason to be in touch every four to six months. I always found the nature of his calls amusing, whether it was comparing the interests of our daughters who are about the same age or asking me to read a speech. One call that I found particularly interesting was his request for me to find a place to live for an employee who experienced a house fire. Later I came to know that within his team he had people who could have performed all these functions; these were just ways for him to stay in touch with me.

Twenty-five years into our relationship, I received a call asking for something very specific. My friend indicated that he had sold one of his companies and was not going to distribute the proceeds. Instead he was going to invest in diversified assets and create new entrepreneurs, leveraging his capital into new financing opportunities. "I need someone who can evaluate real estate projects, do commercial business valuations, and review and negotiate legal documents," he explained to me. Over the years we have shared many laughs together, so I jokingly said, "When do I start?" At that point he said, "Let me get back to you," and abruptly hung up the phone. Five minutes later, I received a phone call from his attorney saying that he was asked to give me a call to negotiate my joining the team. This came as a total shock to me because I was only joking!

At this point in my career I had joined an economic development agency doing meaningful work and was not looking for a career change. Plus, I was a bit uneasy about working for a long-term mentor and friend. I discussed it with my wife and met with him and the board, but having a better understanding still did not make me more comfortable.

As I continued to deliberate, my wife and I received a phone call from my daughter who had relocated to Washington, DC. She wanted us to come hear her new pastor. As we drove to DC, my wife discussed the opportunity further. "Have you prayed about it?" she asked pointedly.

"Yes," I said, "but let me tell you what I prayed. I said, 'Lord, you're gonna have to have someone literally tell me this is the right thing for me to do.'"

When we arrived at the church that Sunday morning, we learned that the sermon would be given by a guest minister. As he began his opening remarks, he indicated he had been led to change his message for the day.

"There are those of you here," he began, "who are questioning the increase that God has planned for you. 'Now he that ministereth seed to the sower both minister bread for your food, and mul-

tiply your seed sown, and increase the fruits of your righteousness'"
(2 Corinthians 9:10 KJV).

That was the first time my wife elbowed me in the side, indicating, "He's talking to you."

His next point was "You cannot plow your new field looking back at the old field you've already plowed," and he quoted Luke 9:62: "No man, having put his hand to the plough, and looking back, is fit for the kingdom of God" (KJV). Another elbow jab.

Then the visiting pastor made the point of leaning not to your own understanding but trusting in God, citing Proverbs 3:5–6: "Trust in the Lord with all thine heart; and lean not unto thine own understanding. In all thy ways acknowledge him, and he shall direct thy paths" (KJV).

With this set of elbow jabs I began to bruise, but the point had been made.

What are the odds that my daughter would call at the last minute, ask that we come to her church service that weekend? What are the odds that, unannounced, the senior pastor would not deliver the message and that a guest minister would? What are the odds that the guest minister would address an issue specific to the questions that I had raised? Divine intervention!

That evening I called my longtime friend and said, "I don't know where this is going, but I'm on board. Let's figure it out." My new journey has exceeded my wildest dreams. My occasional mentor has now become my friend, and I am honored now to serve him, not as a customer but as a valued member of his team! You never know what opportunities await when you are able to contribute as much to your mentor as he is able to contribute to you.

14
IN UNEXPECTED PLACES
Dr. Henry Allen

From one man he made all the nations, that they should inhabit the whole earth; and he marked out their appointed times in history and the boundaries of their lands.
ACTS 17:26

My spiritual journey in Christ and His kingdom went across unknown destinations to unexpected mentors as I left the friendly confines of my youthful Black community to enter the evangelical orbit. On August 14, 1971, the love we had was forever shattered as my family moved to Pembroke, Illinois—a rural location rife with poverty and isolated social spaces. To be sure, I detested the move. Yet, the Lord caused me to thrive in the valley of disappointment. I excelled even more during high school while my family situation devolved, deteriorating to a crisis point when my drunken father kicked me out of his residence a month before my high school graduation. All told, these were the coldest days of my life. Nonetheless, weeping may endure for a night, but it explodes in the morning with fantastic joy. The Lord was then preparing me for ultimate success in the White evangelical world as well as within the dominant culture.

Abandoned by my family at age seventeen, I was invited to live with a White evangelical family at a Bible camp in my unforeseen crisis. Dave and Sharon Williams (with their small children) were graduates of Wheaton College, working at the Bible Witness Camp (BWC) in St. Anne, Illinois. On May 5, 1973, I began my sojourn into unknown social spaces, living and working at the BWC. It was definitely a culture shock, but I was desperate, having neither funds nor choice. Urgent necessity was truly the mother of innovation!

From my years at the BWC, I learned and taught the Bible rigorously, starting a daily habit of biblical meditations in journals that I have continued until this day. Dave was a carpenter who taught the book of Proverbs as the lead Sunday school teacher. He grew up at the camp where his father was the pastor and camp director. His mother and five siblings also resided in this African American community, where the children attended the local schools. The adult camp staff was White, while the congregants were Black—mainly poor with very rural mindsets. Across my tenure, I taught the Bible to classes from kindergarten to eighth grade. I served in the Awana program (a Christian youth program based on Bible memory and fun, competitive games), worked on the maintenance staff, and assisted Dave in his carpentry business. These were rugged times living with the Williams family, and I thought that they would never end. It was for me, at the time, a type of purgatory. I petitioned the Lord regularly for deliverance to new horizons, away from those very isolated country roads full of trailer homes.

I was unaware that the Lord was shaping me for future service. Dave and Sharon sent me to college at Southern Illinois University Carbondale for my freshman year. They were the conduit for my matriculation to Wheaton College, thereby socializing me to the cultural intricacies of White evangelicalism. I learned to study the Bible proficiently under their tutelage, while enjoying their hospitality and benefiting from their sacrifices. As I finished undergraduate study, the entire BWC experience nurtured me.

What did I learn? I learned well to move beyond petty ethnocentrism and racist proclivities in my life. I learned to cherish the poor and needy, despite the associated challenges. I learned to work hard and cherish every opportunity to shine for the Lord. To my surprise, I was eventually awarded a Danforth Graduate Fellowship, being accepted for doctoral study at the University of Chicago. Everything had worked together for my good. After sowing in tears, I reaped with great joy because I met my darling wife, Juliet (a Liberian), because of my attendance at the Bible Witness Camp. Truly, the Lord guides in mysterious ways. He poignantly proved and explicated Acts 17:26 in my life's journey: "From one man he made all the nations, that they should inhabit the whole earth; and he marked out their appointed times in history and the boundaries of their lands."

The Lord led me to circumstances I detested, in a culture that was both unfamiliar and uncomfortable, to shape my life, marriage, family, and ministry. His wisdom is always best, even in the toughest of times (see Romans 8:28). Like Daniel in Babylon, my journey has produced awe and worship before the Lord of Hosts.

> Praise be to the name of God for ever and ever;
>   wisdom and power are his.
> He changes times and seasons;
>   he deposes kings and raises up others.
> He gives wisdom to the wise
>   and knowledge to the discerning.
> He reveals deep and hidden things;
>   he knows what lies in darkness,
>   and light dwells with him.
> I thank and praise you, God of my ancestors:
>   You have given me wisdom and power,
> you have made known to me what we asked of you,
>   you have made known to us the dream of the
>   king.   (Daniel 2:20–23)

Never despise small beginnings.

15

SOMETIMES YOU HAVE TO GO TO THEM

Rev. Odell Cleveland

For I know the thoughts that I think toward you,
saith the LORD, thoughts of peace, and not of evil,
to give you an expected end.
JEREMIAH 29:11 KJV

In the fall of 2007, I was at a gas station and ran into Ishmael Hinson, a young man who had played on my son's high school basketball team. I had watched and cheered for him the past year while attending practices and games, so I asked him how college was going.

He said, "Oh, it didn't work out," the shame noticeable in his eyes. "But I'm doing fine. Playin' ball."

I handed him my business card and asked him to call me, because I knew in my spirit that he was falling in with the wrong crowd. He never called, so I had my son find him and bring him to my office.

> When Jesus came back to Capernaum a few days later, it was heard that He was at home. And many were gathered together, so that there was no longer space, not even near the door; and He was speaking the word to them. And some people came, bringing to Him a man who was paralyzed, carried by four

65

men. And when they were unable to get to Him because of the crowd, they removed the roof above Him; and after digging an opening, they let down the pallet on which the paralyzed man was lying. (Mark 2:1–4 NASB)

It's usually not enough to tell someone "Just give me a call" and hope for the best. Sometimes, you have to be more aggressive. In the story conveyed in the gospel of Mark, these friends of a paralyzed man knew that there was only One who could heal him. They were not passive. They didn't ask Jesus to come to him. They acted and brought him to Jesus. The result? Jesus healed him by commanding him to "get up, pick up your pallet, and go home" (v. 11 NASB).

I met with this young man and mentored him for six years. Over time, he grew from being a college dropout going down the wrong path to obtaining an undergrad communications degree from North Carolina Central University in 2013, spending a summer at the New York Film Academy, and earning a master's degree from the University of Memphis in 2019.

I remember the day I received a call that President Barack Obama wanted to encourage businesses nationwide to provide summer jobs to low-income youth, and wanted to bring sterling examples of what worked to the White House. I decided to bring Ish. He had a blast, and the experience changed his life. He sat ten feet from President Obama, shook hands with rock-music artist Jon Bon Jovi, talked for thirty minutes with then Labor Secretary Hilda Solis, and sent emails to everyone he met when he returned home.

Today, Ish is a sports-and-media rights agent at Creative Artists Agency, traveling the world representing talent. One of my proudest moments was when Ish was asked to serve as a panelist at Duke University School of Law's Sports and Entertainment Law Society Symposium.

Always be sensitive to God's voice. If your heart beats with compassion for someone, act on that heartbeat and reach out. Then watch God give the increase.

16

AN UNEXPECTED BLESSING

Rev. Dr. Noel Hutchinson

Timothy, my son, I am giving you this command in keeping with the prophecies once made about you, so that by recalling them you may fight the battle well, holding on to faith and a good conscience, which some have rejected and so have suffered shipwreck with regard to the faith.
1 TIMOTHY 1:18–19

After becoming a licensed preacher, I was faithful to my church, Bethesda Baptist in New Rochelle, New York. I sang in the choirs and shadowed my pastor, Dr. Allen Paul Weaver Jr., everywhere. After I accepted my call, I made it my business to be supportive and learn everything I could. Because I had a flexible work schedule, I made it to every funeral and even occasionally did Bible study and an evening youth worship service.

On one particular Sunday Pastor Weaver was preaching away from his home church. Earlier that week he met with me and Deacon Chairman Dennis Cummins in his office. He told me that I was the worship leader and Deacon Cummins would supervise. That Sunday, as I took my place at the front of the church, Deacon Cummins waved to the pulpit and directed me to run worship. I was comfortable, as I had done this as early as my college days.

The preacher that Sunday was Rev. Richard C. Gay, who served for twenty-four years as Dr. Gardner C. Taylor's right-hand man at

Concord Baptist Church in Brooklyn, New York. When Dr. Taylor was at the height of his ministry, traveling around the world, Rev. Gay kept things moving at Concord. After worship, Rev. Gay approached me. He said, "Young man, you did a fabulous job. You're going places, and I'm gonna help you."

Rev. Gay kept his promise. I made it my business on Mondays to attend the Baptist Ministers' Conference of New York and Vicinity, the largest gathering of its type in the country. I would see him every week and fellowship with him, my pastor, and the other preachers after the meeting over lunch. As a young minister, I listened and soaked up knowledge. These preachers were supportive when I began seminary, and several of them were on my ordination council. Through them I received numerous preaching opportunities. At the forefront of this was Richard Gay.

In May 1991, I stood in front of Convent Baptist Church, a recent seminary graduate looking for a pastorate. Richard Gay, after greeting me, said, "I know you just graduated from Drew and you're about to get married. I know of an opportunity. Gary Simpson is looking for an associate at Concord. He has his eyes on an old man, but I told him he needs a young man. I'll put in a good word for you."

A month later I was a summer intern at Concord. Two months later, while driving with Dr. Gary Simpson over the Brooklyn Bridge, he said, "Start looking for an apartment in Brooklyn . . . You're now one of the pastors at Concord."

Concord Baptist Church of Brooklyn is one of the best-known Black Baptist churches in the world. When I arrived it was a ten-thousand-member church, with twenty-three nonprofit ministries covering the gamut of urban needs. Its pastor emeritus was Dr. Gardner C. Taylor, arguably the best preacher of the last one hundred years. And now I would contribute in some way to this legacy, all because of an unexpected encounter with a seasoned clergyman.

First Timothy 1:18–19 shows us how an older minister can speak life into a younger one, as a reminder that God entrusts great things to them. The apostle Paul also tells the young minister to hold "on to faith and a good conscience" in the fulfillment of ministry. To lose focus is to invite shipwreck of one's faith and witness. For me, Richard Gay stood as a reminder of what could happen when one remains faithful to what God placed in them. God has a way of placing people in your life who are conduits, who help bring things to pass in your life.

Who is your conduit? And who are you a conduit for?

17
BE CAREFUL WHAT YOU SAY
Dr. Lee N. June

My dear brothers and sisters, take note of this:
Everyone should be quick to listen, slow to speak and
slow to become angry, because human anger does not
produce the righteousness that God desires.
JAMES 1:19–20

As I was growing up, and before I was aware of James's admonition, this concept was uttered by my parents and other mentors in the form of expressions such as "Count to ten before you speak," "An empty wagon makes a lot of noise," and "You need to wash your mouth with soap." These were all aimed at helping us to be measured in speech and not speak too quickly. In other words, we were being told to "be careful what you say."

We often too quickly express opinions or give our viewpoints on a subject matter or topic of discussion. Rather than following James's advice, we make a mockery of his saying and invent our own. We become "swift to speak, quick to become angry, and slow to hear," as James warned.

Over the years, I have learned how important this passage in James is as I have seen others follow its dictates. It is a principle we should all follow. Many of the people who have been my mentors have followed this principle. This has in particular been extremely

71

helpful to me when it comes to leadership or administrative positions.

When I mentor others, I attempt to walk with them in their life journey, to encourage them, and to give practical advice. This is what mentees want. Likewise, James offers much practical advice in this epistle.

What can happen when we violate James's admonition? We can utter words that do not accurately fit the situation because we spoke before we received all the information necessary to make an informed comment. We might say things that we wish we had not said. Words spoken and heard can never be unheard, apologies notwithstanding. The adage that "sticks and stones may break my bones, but names do not hurt me" does not apply to everyone. Words do wound, and wounds may be deep and long-lasting. While we might eventually learn how to not let words hurt us, this is not easily achieved.

Additionally, when we violate James's principle, anger may overtake us. In anger, we violate another biblical mandate: "'In your anger do not sin:' Do not let the sun go down while you are still angry, and do not give the devil a foothold" (Ephesians 4:26–27). Thus, rather than become problem-solvers, we do things that lead to division.

In mentoring, we want our mentees to be the best persons that they can be. Helping them to see how words can be healing is just as important as helping them to see how words can do the opposite.

Think about a recent situation in which you were slow to listen, quick to speak, and quick to become angry. What was the impact of this behavior on others? Upon you?

Now think of a recent situation in which you were quick to listen, slow to speak, and slow to become angry. What was the impact of this behavior on others? Upon you? What might you begin to do, starting today, to better align yourself to James's admonition and make it a regular part of your lifestyle?

Mentees are not just watching what we do; they are also watching what we say. Just as you are careful to model good behavior, be all the more careful to model good speech—demonstrating that there is "a time to keep silence, and a time to speak" (Ecclesiastes 3:7 KJV).

18

JESUS AS MENTOR

Rev. C. Jeffrey Wright

Think of yourselves the way Christ Jesus thought of himself. He had equal status with God but didn't think so much of himself that he had to cling to the advantages of that status no matter what.

PHILIPPIANS 2:5–6 MSG

Did you ever want to be famous, or the boss, or just in charge of things? What is it about that promotion you want that is really driving you? Money, status, or some other perk? If you are the manager on your job or if you even want to be the manager, what is it that really motivates you?

Movies, books, and other media often focus on those who are kings, presidents, leaders, and others in charge. The idea of being the person who is able to make the rules, control others, and have responsibility for the way things work is very appealing to many. The perks and benefits of leadership are often depicted as special privileges, larger portions, greater freedoms, and the seeming happiness of having it all and needing nothing.

The movies and media depictions of the all-powerful leader who has become obsessed to the point of destructive behavior have had a tremendous impact on our world and on our own society. The truth is that the more self-centered the power, the more isolated and alone the leader becomes as others seek only what this self-centered leader has and wants. Truth is out of the picture as the people being led say and do only what the leader wants until the leader is alone in a prison of lies of his own making.

But the adage that "with great power comes great responsibility" should bring balance to those thoughts and desires. The greatest benefit of leadership should not be for the leader but for those who are led.

Think about this: a leader is also a mentor. What kind of mentor is leading *you*?

God's ways are so very different from our own. The essence of God's expression of *servant* leadership is this: from His position as leader of the universe, He chose to serve all His creation by coming to be with us as Jesus Christ. Some leaders have learned in the workplace that the practice of walking around and engaging directly with those doing the work is an effective practice. Identifying with those who work for you, remembering when you were "one of them," and gathering firsthand the information that can only be known by those on the front lines make for more effective leadership and more effective service. The people close to the action really know what is going on. The Bible makes it clear that God Himself gained that benefit from His time with us on earth and "understands our weaknesses since he had the same temptations we do, though he never once gave way to them and sinned" (Hebrews 4:15 TLB).

The power of humility is that it helps you to become a better leader, or mentor, because you become more knowledgeable and more attuned to the needs of others. When you understand what people need through experiencing life the way they experience it, empathy and compassion result. This increases your connection with others, raises their self-esteem, and gives you direction and vision to use the power of leadership to create more satisfying lives for others. The extreme opposite of this is narcissism, behavior that is self-centered to an extreme and at the expense of others.

The serving leader brings blessings because he has experienced the life of those being led and knows the benefit of blessing others. Paul encourages us in Philippians 2 to imitate Christ in this way.

Though He had all the power of the universe, He came and lived with us, giving up all of His status and privilege to serve us and save us.

So, what kind of mentor are you? Even more, what kind of mentor discipled you in your walk with Christ? If they did not follow Jesus's example . . . you may need to look to Jesus Himself as your example. His is the pathway to empathetic, successful leadership.

19
WALKING WITH WAYNE
Rev. Arthur Jackson

As iron sharpens iron, so one person sharpens another.
PROVERBS 27:17

"That's a good question!" Over the fifteen-plus years I've known Wayne, I've heard him utter that statement scores of times. It's the kind of statement that coaches and mentors like to hear. Something they've said has grabbed their protégé's attention, and with that the possibility for progress has gone to the next level.

When Wayne, his wife, and their two sons came to the church I pastored in 2006, it was to fulfill the internship requirements of his seminary coursework. Though he held an MBA from a prominent university and was savvy in business, his call to ministry was stronger than the attraction of a successful business career.

From the start Wayne was eager and energetic. Upon the completion of his degree program, he and his family relocated to the Detroit area where he assumed a ministry position on staff with the church he had left when he entered seminary. But distance did not squelch our relationship. Over time we grew even closer.

Wayne welcomed a voice of reason, wisdom, and experience into his life. He recognized the value of journeying with someone who had traveled where he was going. Wayne's value to his local church and the Lord's work in general became increasingly apparent to me and others.

Paul had a relationship with several leaders who were his junior.

One of those was Timothy. His relationship with Timothy started on Paul's second missionary journey and developed from there. Timothy's trustworthiness was exceptional.

> I hope in the Lord Jesus to send Timothy to you soon. . . . I have no one else like him, who will show genuine concern for your welfare. . . . But you know that Timothy has proved himself, because as a son with his father he has served with me in the work of the gospel. (Philippians 2:19–20, 22)

Eventually Timothy was assigned to local church ministry in Ephesus. That's where he was when Paul wrote these words:

> Do not neglect your gift, which was given you through prophecy when the body of elders laid their hands on you.
> Be diligent in these matters; give yourself wholly to them, so that everyone may see your progress. Watch your life and doctrine closely. Persevere in them, because if you do, you will save both yourself and your hearers. (1 Timothy 4:14–16)

Wayne is the kind of person who invites conversation partners, and over the years we have talked regularly. Sometimes pride and ego compel us to silence, muffle, or not even invite other voices into our lives. Do you have a conversation partner? Someone who you're in conversation with? People who allow you to think and talk out loud? Who ask "Have you thought about . . ." questions? Who help you process direction and timing and risks? Who help you evaluate gifts and calling? Within the last eighteen months or so, my conversations with Wayne have considered such things. They are worthwhile, important conversations.

The pandemic, the cultural confusion that includes racial tensions, and the closer evaluation of pastoral gifts have led Wayne to conclude that his season for local church pastoral ministry has come and gone. Another door for usefulness has opened wide and Wayne has walked through it. Because Wayne has had me and others on the journey with him, he is confident that the path that he is on is the right one.

Where do you find your feet now? Who's walking with you? Is someone asking you questions that make you ponder your goals and your path? If you don't have that kind of person—who can you invite? What are you waiting on?

20

THE CHURCH AS MENTOR

Rev. Dr. Noel Hutchinson

We who are strong ought to bear with the failings of the weak and not to please ourselves. Each of us should please our neighbors for their good, to build them up. For even Christ did not please himself but, as it is written: "The insults of those who insult you have fallen on me." For everything that was written in the past was written to teach us, so that through the endurance taught in the Scriptures and the encouragement they provide we might have hope.

ROMANS 15:1–4

James (not his real name), an eighteen-year-old African American, was the older of two boys raised by a single mother in the Albany, New York, housing projects. Society normally dictates that success passes by this type of household.

But the Black Church has always been an incubator for its members, continually giving hope and opportunity in communities where they are in short supply. The Concord Baptist Church in Brooklyn, New York, mentored James, who, along with his family, was active in the church. As James made his way through high school, his future was unclear. He didn't connect well with school, as is the case with many youth in his circumstances; his grades were marginal at best. Yet he tried because Concord made education a priority. With that indoctrination, James avoided some of the urban challenges right outside his apartment.

In 1992 I was a staff pastor at Concord. Our senior pastor, Dr. Gary Simpson, entrusted me with finding a firm to overhaul the sound system for our three-thousand-seat sanctuary. After nine months of heavy research along with bids, we chose a firm. During the summer installation, some of our youth volunteered to help. James was one of them. As it was my project, I welcomed them. During this time, the sound firm showed the youth how to operate the system. In a short amount of time, James could operate it as well as the sound professionals could. They marveled at his innate abilities, and he became so proficient that when we had issues with the sound during worship, Dr. Simpson, I, and some of the members would ask, "Where's James?" The wunderkind did work-arounds while running the sound system better than many who had worked with sound systems for years. The sound firm, which also worked for Broadway shows, was impressed and had James work with them as a summer intern, promising him a job when he graduated high school.

However, there was a problem. James had been cutting classes and was on the verge of being tossed out of school. One day I had to stand as his advocate in an official setting. When we got outside, I said to James in front of his mother, "No one is asking you to make the honor roll; just graduate! Please!" I reminded him of the opportunity that he was about to lose if he didn't. His mother looked at James when I finished and said a forceful "Amen."

I left Concord in early 1995 to begin pastoring in Memphis, Tennessee. I had hoped that James would graduate before I left, but he didn't. The sound firm still allowed him to work as an apprentice. I was nervous that he would cause this opportunity to evaporate. Around June, Dr. Simpson called me, sharing that James had graduated, joined the sound engineers' union, and landed a job as a sound engineer with the Dance Theatre of Harlem. He then said James would start work in Amsterdam the next week. The church paid for his expedited passport so he could go. Dr. Simpson called me because of how I had encouraged James while I was in Brooklyn; Dr. Simpson wanted me to know. I was ecstatic! I then talked to Deacons

Joe Dallas and Bernard Clapp, also key parts of this story, and you could hear the pride over the phone as they said, "Our boy did it!"

In 2000, the Dance Theatre of Harlem was in town. I attended the event, and as much as I enjoyed the performance, I sat and cried tears of joy as I privately thanked God for allowing me to be a part of this story.

The admonition of Paul in Romans 15 speaks to the strengthening of community by us lifting each other up. It speaks to mentorship because, while strong now, we have been weak, and we are implored to help those in need. In the end, we individually and collectively become stronger. This is the legacy of the Black Church. When one makes it, all the members rejoice, because we intrinsically understand the value of community. When we remember this, and continue that legacy, we will recite more success stories like this one you just read. And ultimately God will get the glory through us.

21
CONTINUE
Rev. Reginald M. Holiday

But as for you, continue in what you have learned and have firmly believed, knowing from whom you learned it.
2 TIMOTHY 3:14 ESV

Mentors understand that they are passing on something that should have an ongoing impact even after the mentor is no longer around. They make deposits into us for our trust and stewardship (1 Timothy 6:20; 2 Timothy 1:12, 14). How blessed we are to have those who impart things that shape and steer us even without those mentors. As mentees, we are responsible for continuing what we have learned and apprehended from those who mentored us.

Bishop Ithiel Conrad Clemmons, my first pastor and senior leader of the historic Wells Memorial Church, was this type of mentor to me. At Wells Memorial, he taught me key spiritual disciplines, ministry protocols, and practices. I was allowed to teach, preach, and train others. I learned to "discharge all the duties of [my] ministry" (2 Timothy 4:5). My theology was founded and framed under his watchful eye in the rich tradition of the African American Pentecostal Holiness Church.

The Father saw that I sat at the feet of one of those who had sat before many of our unheralded faith pioneers. Since Pastor Ithiel Clemmons was a national church historian, I had the unique opportunity to meet those about whom little is written but who have made enormous contributions to the kingdom of God. I heard stories of the incredible Holy Spirit outpouring at the Azusa Street Revival at the turn of the century, a movement I like to call the "Third Great Awakening." An African American man, Rev. William Seymour, was used by God to shatter the boundaries of race and class and gather Black and White to worship and minister together as a body. I was taught of the founding of the Church of God in Christ and how the Lord initiated this work under the leadership of its founder, Charles Harrison Mason, who was present at Azusa. I was exposed to, inspired by, and influenced by African American theologians such as James Cone, Howard Thurman, Cain Hope Felder, C. Eric Lincoln, and J. Deotis Roberts. I was tutored through the teachings of great men such as Frederick Douglass, W. E. B. Du Bois, Martin Luther King Jr., and John Perkins. Mine would be the privilege of having hands laid on me in times of ordination and impartation by men who had the hands of Bishop Charles Harrison Mason laid on them.

My experience included eclectic training under Bishop Clemmons's tutelage. I was exposed to Rabbi Abraham Heschel, James Stewart, Halford Luccock, Alan Redpath, and many more! Even in the African American Church, I was exposed to White European theologians and their thinking. I had to be. The landscape required it. I was blessed to engage with many of the brightest upcoming theological minds of the mid and late nineties and early two thousands. Under Bishop (as I lovingly referred to him), I was immersed more and more in the work of racial reconciliation in the church. And yet, somehow, I perceived there was so much more! I could not articulate it or define it, but I knew there was more.

In December 1998, I spoke to Bishop Clemmons one last time, communicating through his wife, Mrs. Clara Clemmons. Bishop was near death. His words to me were simple yet profound and continue to guide me to this day. He said, "You know what to do. Just continue to do that."

As I prayed and pondered his words, I recalled what Paul wrote to his spiritual son Timothy. "But as for you, continue in what you have

22
CAUGHT RATHER THAN TAUGHT

Rev. Dr. Noel Hutchinson

Therefore if you have any encouragement from being united with Christ, if any comfort from his love, if any common sharing in the Spirit, if any tenderness and compassion, then make my joy complete by being like-minded, having the same love, being one in spirit and of one mind. Do nothing out of selfish ambition or vain conceit. Rather, in humility value others above yourselves, not looking to your own interests but each of you to the interests of the others.

PHILIPPIANS 2:1–4

I often reminisce about the beginnings of my time in ministry. Many of my fondest memories from those formative years are of mentorship that was "caught rather than taught." One recollection is meeting Rev. Dr. Wyatt T. Walker. He was larger than life to me. I grew up reading about him in *Ebony* magazine, as he worked with Dr. Martin Luther King Jr. before becoming the pastor of Canaan Baptist Church in Harlem, in the same association as my home church. Whenever I would talk to him, I would reference the association connection and my pastor, and it would cause him to remember who I was.

However, my favorite memory was the first time I met him. At that time, he was arguably at the strength of his power. His work at Canaan was flourishing, and he was writing books at a blistering pace. This was in the late 1980s, probably around 1987. I was a licentiate. No title. No cachet. No résumé. Fury with no fire. Noise with no rhythm. I started a conversation with Dr. Walker—I think it was about seminary, which I was considering. He was totally focused on me.

All of a sudden, someone who knew him much better than I did walked up and started talking to him. They said no more than five words before he stopped them and then said something like this: "Excuse me . . . Can't you see that I'm talking to this young man? Please don't interrupt. We will talk after I'm through with him." Keep in mind that Dr. Walker was always smooth, and he seldom raised his voice. I was in pleasant shock. By then I had seen the best and what I perceived as some of the worst of those who were in the clergy. We finished our conversation, and he wished me well.

In another instance, I met Dr. Calvin Butts, pastor of Abyssinian Baptist Church. My pastor encouraged me to talk to him about seminary, as he had gone to Union and Drew Seminaries. Not knowing me but giving me a listening ear, he helped me to shape my decision to go to Drew. I've known him now for more than thirty years and have been able to personally thank him for this advice and other things he's done for people I know and love.

Dr. Butts's predecessor at Abyssinian, Dr. Samuel DeWitt Proctor, also had a part to play in my story. He preached one night at Mount Olive Baptist Church in Hackensack, New Jersey, where I was youth minister. Dr. Proctor was in the pastor's study with me and Rev. Gregory Jackson. Rev. Jackson told Dr. Proctor that Concord Baptist Church in Brooklyn was considering me for staff pastor. Dr. Proctor then said, "You'll be perfect . . . They will love you with your big voice and measured tone, because that's a big sanctuary. You'll do well there." It must have been prophetic because a few months later it came to pass.

In every case there was no compelling reason for them to pour into me, even briefly. Gentlemen like these taught me humility. If you have to brag about who you are, then maybe you're not that great. Our text in Philippians 2:1–4 stresses love of each other through community, with one spirit and one mind. Being humble while concerned about others helps to enhance those around you.

God blessed me with a ministry that has spanned the globe, but the beginning embers came from giants who were willing to model humility while helping me. As great as they were—in Dr. Butts's case, he still is—they always were accessible. It's a lesson I've tried to emulate throughout my ministry.

23
FROM ZEAL TO KNOWLEDGE
Rev. Reginald M. Holiday

Meanwhile a Jew named Apollos, a native of Alexandria, came to Ephesus. He was a learned man, with a thorough knowledge of the Scriptures. He had been instructed in the way of the Lord, and he spoke with great fervor and taught about Jesus accurately, though he knew only the baptism of John. He began to speak boldly in the synagogue. When Priscilla and Aquila heard him, they invited him to their home and explained to him the way of God more adequately.

When Apollos wanted to go to Achaia, the brothers and sisters encouraged him and wrote to the disciples there to welcome him. When he arrived, he was a great help to those who by grace had believed. For he vigorously refuted his Jewish opponents in public debate, proving from the Scriptures that Jesus was the Messiah.

ACTS 18:24–28

After my wife, Linda, and I were born again, I recall how George and Darlene East took us, along with a host of others, under their wings to disciple us. This amazing man of God and his devout and intelligent wife poured so much into us to help us become quality Christians and leaders of God's people. They would spend time with us, sharing their spiritual and personal experience, helping to prepare us for what we had no idea was coming in the Lord. We were so eager. We had a lot of zeal but not much knowledge. Yet they were willing and patient with us not only to answer our many questions but also to nurture us in areas we had no knowledge of. In a sense, what Aquila and Priscilla were to Apollos, the Easts were to us.

There are plenty of examples of zealous individuals in the Bible who were tempered and matured in the mentoring process. Consider Peter, one of Jesus's key disciples. He was, as the Bible describes, a man rough around the edges—one who blurted out whatever he was thinking and also acted on impulse. One fateful day, as Jesus was drawing closer to the time of his crucifixion, Peter had a violent encounter with the enemies of his Lord:

> Again [Jesus] asked them, "Who is it you want?"
>
> "Jesus of Nazareth," they said.
>
> Jesus answered, "I told you that I am he. If you are looking for me, then let these men go." This happened so that the words he had spoken would be fulfilled: "I have not lost one of those you gave me."
>
> Then Simon Peter, who had a sword, drew it and struck the high priest's servant, cutting off his right ear. (The servant's name was Malchus.)
>
> Jesus commanded Peter, "Put your sword away! Shall I not drink the cup the Father has given me?" (John 18:7–11)

Jesus had to calm Peter down! He had zeal but needed tempering. Peter needed to see how the circumstances lined up so well with the will of God that he did not need to intervene with his human solution to what he saw as Jesus's problem. He would learn much more in the days to come.

We can also take a look at Samuel. His mother, Hannah, dedicated him to the Lord and sent him away at the tender age of three to the temple to be mentored by the priest Eli. One night as he lay in his bed, Samuel heard a voice. In his eagerness to please his mentor, he immediately went to Eli to ask why he was being summoned. But Eli had not summoned him. After three such incidents, Eli realized that it was the Lord who was calling Samuel, and he counseled Samuel to answer the Lord directly. Samuel was obedient to the counsel, and as a result became Israel's first prophet (1 Samuel 3).

Solomon mentored the Queen of Sheba, a woman eager to know this man whom she had heard so much about. As a result, she returned to her people with the knowledge of God and the gift of wisdom. That gift kept on giving through the centuries, as Ethiopia is one of the earliest places that helped to grow monotheism in its Judaic and Christian forms.

Like Apollos, Peter, Samuel, and the Queen of Sheba were willing and eager mentees. While they had a level of giftedness and intelligence, they had one trait that made them special: they were teachable. Luke writes concerning Apollos that he was "an eloquent man" and "proficient in the Scriptures" (Acts 18:24 NASB). Apollos had been instructed in the way of the Lord. Though he was fervent in spirit while speaking and accurately teaching the things of the Lord, something was missing! God used Aquila and Priscilla to take him aside and accurately explain to Apollos the way of God. How powerful is that?

It was after their mentoring that Apollos was able to advance in his ministry call. Likewise, through Elder George and Darlene East's mentoring, Linda and I could move much further in the Lord than we had ever imagined. The Lord saw our readiness, just like He had with Apollos, and then the right teachers (mentors) appeared.

I encourage every young person to open themselves to the right mentor. You don't have to make the journey alone or only learn from your own mistakes. Believe God for that person or persons who will help you grow and become more of what He wants you to be—by directing and harnessing your zeal for life and godliness into a solid life-message and testimony!

24
SEE THE BIGGER PICTURE
Rev. Reginald M. Holiday

Then Jesus came to them and said, "All authority in heaven and on earth has been given to me. Therefore go and make disciples of all nations, baptizing them in the name of the Father and of the Son and of the Holy Spirit, and teaching them to obey everything I have commanded you. And surely I am with you always, to the very end of the age."
MATTHEW 28:18–20

Jesus had an enlarged vision. When He said this to His disciples, He expanded their view of what was possible in the earth. Before He engaged with them, not one had probably traveled more than a hundred miles from where they had been born. But with this enlarged vision that Jesus gave, they traveled to Italy, Greece, Ethiopia, Lebanon, Turkey, even Spain!

In most of our development and growth, it is easy to become limited by what we know or have experienced. I believe this is one of the places where a great mentor can help us move beyond that and into the more important things we can be and achieve.

Our Lord Jesus Christ took a ragtag bunch of Jewish men who likely had not ventured much farther than where they were born and raised and exposed them to ministry with global proportions. He knew that for His Father's ultimate aim to have a global family of sons and daughters just like Jesus to be fulfilled, these disciples would have to see the bigger picture. Each time He spoke to them as His ascension drew nearer, He urged them to go global with the gospel and see this small nucleus of faithful souls become a worldwide family to the glory of God.

That's what mentors do. They urge us on in seeing and pursuing things greater than we imagine or believe possible for us. Jesus Christ exhorted His band of devoted followers to see the endless possibilities which He entrusted to them.

As a mentor of sorts to His disciples, Jesus expressed His full support of His mentees and gave them clear instructions on how to reach what He saw in them. He also promised to be there with them. This kind of commitment blesses those who are being mentored. Mentees need to know that there are those pulling for their success who provide wise counsel and who will not abandon them along the way. Our Lord Jesus Christ had poured into His disciples, and now it was their turn, and He had to ensure they did not play it small. His words to them were a charge to live into the bigness of what God had ordained for them to be and do. We all need people in our lives like that! Amen?

Being blessed to have a host of mentors throughout the years, I remember two in particular helped me see that what I was called to was more significant than I thought. The first of these was my beloved grandmother, Lula Mae Hill. She was the quintessential grandma, a Southern church lady who saw the good in everyone and always had something encouraging to say. In her wise way, she encouraged me to see beyond my immediate context. That's one of the things that quality mentors do! They help mentees see and believe beyond their current selves. They expose us to opportunities and experiences beyond what we have known and challenge us to press into our potential. Grandma Mae was an expert at doing this!

The second mentor, Apostle Otis Lockett, helped me see the bigger picture. God used this iconic servant of the Lord to stretch my vision and to increase my confidence in His call on my life. Apostle Lockett told me one day, "Holiday, your ministry is larger than the local church you lead. Don't limit yourself to that." Mentors help us most by enabling us to see the capability we don't see ourselves, or fear expressing. Mentors increase our vision, encourage our faith, and cheer us on to more extraordinary things.

If you are praying for and seeking quality mentorship, ask for those who will enlarge your perspective to see the bigger picture. You will need those who can show you how to unlock your God-given potential and not play it small! They are out there. Our world needs those who will push beyond the status quo, boundaries, and limitations. Who knows? You could be the next world changer!

25
WOMEN CAN MENTOR MEN, TOO
Dr. Matthew Parker

> *Now Deborah, a prophetess, the wife of Lappidoth, was judging Israel at that time. She used to sit under the palm tree of Deborah between Ramah and Bethel in the hill country of Ephraim; and the* sons *of Israel went up to her for judgment.*
> JUDGES 4:4–5 NASB *(emphasis added)*

In the summer of 1968, I was a camp counselor at Cedine Bible Camp and Missions in Spring City, Tennessee. I had just finished my second year at Grand Rapids School of the Bible and Music. One aspect of my history plagued my thoughts constantly: I never had a mother who raised me. My mother, Ruth Spann Parker, died just after my brother Gregory was born, when I was about three years of age. I have no memory of her.

What I noticed that summer was that this cook—at the time her name was Barbara Simon, but they called her "Mother Simon"—seemed to be the go-to counselor for all the adults at the camp. The director, the founder, the head cook, and many others, I observed, would find a way to her cabin for counsel. The memory of my mother-absence piqued my curiosity; why were these adults seeking out this woman? Then I thought maybe she had some wisdom for me, too.

One day, I decided to take that walk, too, and ask Mother Simon if I could join this line of adults who looked to her for advice. It wasn't long before I realized that she could fill the mother-void in my life. "Will you be my mother in the faith?" I asked her. Fortunately for me, she agreed.

Over the years, I would visit Mother Simon two or three times a year in her small house in Atlanta, Georgia. We would sit around the kitchen table, eating fried chicken and talking about my life journey. She never minded sharing her journey, too, and she was so honest and real that I felt comfortable telling her things I might not tell anyone else.

What I came to realize was that as I was talking with her, I was learning how to talk to a woman. We men are notorious for not being very good in that department. The common complaint—I'm sure you've heard it—is that we never talk about what's going on inside of our hearts. With Mother Simon, I developed the ability to share my feelings.

As the years went by, Mother Simon continued to invest her faith, her family, and her finances into my life. I so respected her that I gave her the authority to say "yes" or "no" to my life decisions—even when it came time to marry. Yes, I presented Karon, the woman I desired to marry, to her and asked if she would approve. I admit that I was relieved when she gave her blessing.

This ceding of authority to Mother Simon gave me valuable protection and safety. I credit her not only with helping me to relate successfully to my wife but also with paving the way for me to invest in, support, encourage, and partner with women all over the country in their ministry endeavors through the two platforms God has given me: The Global Summit and the Institute for Black Family Development. I have seen many of these women become authors, program directors, and church and ministry leaders. If not for Mama Simon, as I eventually came to call her, these opportunities would have been greatly diminished.

Years later, Mama Simon—now Mama Walton—would suffer a stroke. Her diminished physical abilities meant she had to move to a convalescent home. I kept up my visits especially then, flying down a couple of times every year to see her. We would talk for hours, with me sharing my puddle of wisdom I had learned and her overwhelming me with Niagara Falls–level insights. One day, I confessed to her as I reflected on our beginnings. "I was such a knucklehead," I told her.

"You were," she replied.

In our more than twenty-five-year journey, that was the very first time that she had ever said anything negative about me.

Here is what Mama Walton taught me about mentoring: Be a vehicle of encouragement. Share your resources. Develop the mentees that God gives you. Hold your criticism. Let your mentee discover what they are missing by the richness of your care and concern for them. When you are so invested in another person's life, you can squeeze out the "knucklehead" part by virtue of your transparency, your generosity, and your positive encouragement.

When I reflect on Mama Walton's mentoring of me, I go immediately to Ephesians 4:29: "Do not let any unwholesome talk come out of your mouths, but only what is helpful for building others up according to their needs, that it may benefit those who listen." I thank God that He gave this motherless child such a profound relationship with someone willing to step in and be a mother to me.

26

MENTORED BY MOTHERS
Rev. Arthur Jackson

I am reminded of your sincere faith, which first lived in your grandmother Lois and in your mother Eunice and, I am persuaded, now lives in you also.
2 TIMOTHY 1:5

Because our family lived in my grandparents' home during my early years, our domain included two women who marked me for life—my mother ("Mother") and my grandmother ("Momma"). Their words, touches, and training were foundational to my formation.

More often than we may admit, mothers are our first mentors. It's their impact that actually fits us to be fashioned by others on whom we are more apt to bestow the label "mentor."

In ancient Israel the siblings Moses, Aaron, and Miriam were all leaders. Scripture tells us, "I brought you up out of Egypt and redeemed you from the land of slavery. I sent Moses to lead you, also Aaron and Miriam" (Micah 6:4).

These three, the children of Amram and Jochebed (Numbers 26:59), were products of the same home. The parents are commended for their faith in the book of Hebrews.

> By faith Moses' parents hid him for three months after he was born, because they saw he was no ordinary child, and they were not afraid of the king's edict. (11:23)

In Exodus 2, however, it's the faith exploits of Jochebed that are on display. She not only concocted a plan to protect her little baby Moses from death, but she also, with the help of young daughter Miriam, conceived a strategy to nurse and nurture him in the early years of his life. And it worked!

Before he was educated in Pharaoh's court, Moses's Hebrew mama, a leader in her own right, mothered the child who would be a premier leader of God's people. And guess who witnessed the love and leadership of their mother as she worked her plan? Her children Miriam and Aaron (who was three years old when Moses was born; see Exodus 7:7).

My Christian faith heritage was fostered by my catechism-reciting, hymn-singing grandmother. Momma, who was proudly educated at the Scotia Women's College in Concord, North Carolina, became the wife of a Presbyterian clergyman. She was keen on education and encouraged a love for learning in her grandchildren. Her rich legacy lives on through us.

My mother was tender, caring, and nurturing, like a shepherd— very pastoral. My heart, as a man and as a minister, has the imprint of my mother's loving care. Her perseverance and faithfulness in marriage were exemplary. My parents were married fifty-seven years, but my father did not begin following Jesus until he was fifty-three. My mother endured some challenging years. Prayer and patience paid off.

In Scripture Timothy is commended by Paul as a faithful, trustworthy servant of Jesus.

> I hope in the Lord Jesus to send Timothy to you soon. . . . I have no one else like him, who will show genuine concern for your welfare. For everyone looks out for their own interests, not those of Jesus Christ. But you know that Timothy has proved himself, because as a son with his father he has served with me in the work of the gospel. (Philippians 2:19–22)

Timothy "proved himself." But he didn't get there by himself. The influence that Timothy's mother and grandmother had on this exceptional pastor are duly noted:

> I am reminded of your sincere faith, which first lived in your grandmother Lois and in your mother Eunice and, I am persuaded, now lives in you also. (2 Timothy 1:5)

> But as for you, continue in what you have learned and have become convinced of, because you know those from whom you learned it, and how from infancy you have known the Holy Scriptures, which are able to make you wise for salvation through faith in Christ Jesus. (2 Timothy 3:14–15)

As mentors guide, support, and counsel us, they leave their mark. Sometimes we fail to give credit where it is due. Let's be careful and intentional to acknowledge and applaud mentoring mothers, past and present. Give it up for them whether they share your blood or your name or not. Hats off to the named and unnamed, educated and uneducated, Black, Brown, or White mothers and women who have labored long and hard and have lived honorably. Their legacy will live on for generations when other influencers are forgotten. Indeed, we call them *blessed*. To God be the glory!

27
QUITTING IS NOT AN OPTION
Dr. Michael R. Lyles

*Therefore, since we are surrounded by such a great cloud
of witnesses, let us throw off everything that hinders
and the sin that so easily entangles. And let us run with
perseverance the race marked out for us, fixing our eyes
on Jesus, the pioneer and perfecter of faith. For the joy set
before him he endured the cross, scorning its shame, and
sat down at the right hand of the throne of God. Consider
him who endured such opposition from sinners, so that
you will not grow weary and lose heart.*
HEBREWS 12:1–3

Traditional medical school education involves two years of classroom
study followed by hospital rotations in different specialties under the
supervision of faculty physicians. My first hospital rotation was four
weeks of anesthesiology, supervised by a physician who seemed to
dislike me from the first day. He never smiled or welcomed me to his
clinic, though we worked very closely together. On the second day,
this quickly followed: him questioning whether I was smart enough
to understand what he was telling me to do.

By the third day, he was yelling at me that I was the worst student
that he had ever had and that I was taking up a spot in the class that a
deserving student should have had. He called me lazy because I came
to work only thirty minutes early, at 5 a.m. He called me a testimony

to tokenism by the fourth day and wanted to know what I would do after I flunked out of school. By the fifth day, Friday, I was so angry and upset that I could hardly focus on my work. I had been called every name but the N-word, but assumed that was coming. I was not convinced that I could do medical school if this was what medical training looked like. It felt more like Marine Corps boot camp with my professor as a profane drill sergeant—intent on breaking me down.

Thankfully, I had the weekend off and took the bus home. I told my mother that I was unsure I could handle this. I told her that I was close to getting in a verbal altercation with him and might get kicked out of medical school. She listened patiently and responded in a manner I did not expect.

"If you do anything to get kicked out of medical school, you cannot come back and live here." She then explained that my experience with racist behavior was not something new. She had experienced racism as a nurse when patients refused to let her take care of them. She experienced it as a university professor paid 20 percent less than her White peers of the same academic rank. She reminded me that my father experienced racism when he was accused of stealing a car that he bought while working two jobs. She went down a litany of aunts, uncles, grandparents, and cousins—all who experienced racism more brutal than getting yelled at in an air-conditioned operating room.

She told me that I had a huge "cloud of witnesses" (Hebrews 12:1–3) in my family that understood my experience and these witnesses were pulling and praying for me—but would not tolerate me acting out of my frustrations and quitting. For that "cloud of witnesses," quitting was not an option, for they had been sustained through their suffering by the same God that could sustain me. She lovingly prepared me a meal and sent me back with one request: "Please pray about this—a lot."

Out of that prayer that weekend came a peace in the midst of persecution that helped me to stay focused. I did not return evil for evil with my instructor but instead channeled that anger into studying harder and keeping focused on the calling of God in my life. I ended up making an A in the course. My professor invited me to celebrate by going for a ride in his airplane with him—which, for his safety, I declined.

God used this experience to teach me perseverance, focus, and that I was not just representing myself but a great cloud of family witnesses who had mentored me to this point in my career. I wonder how things would have been different if my mother and my family had welcomed me back home when I was upset and made quitting an option. I would have never learned how to "consider Jesus" and not grow weary and lose heart when "opposed by sinners" with an MD, who assumed the worst about me. My heart did grow faint, but God guided me—through family mentors—to the rock that is higher than I.

> I remain confident of this:
>   I will see the goodness of the LORD
>   in the land of the living. (Psalm 27:13)

> From the ends of the earth I call to you,
>   I call as my heart grows faint;
>   lead me to the rock that is higher than I.
>   (Psalm 61:2)

28

DRAWING OUT THE WATERS

Dr. Henry Allen

The purposes of a person's heart are deep waters,
but one who has insight draws them out.
PROVERBS 20:5

The verse above, from King Solomon, reminds us that the Lord of glory always blesses us with many pivotal relationships that nurture us or develop His treasures of potential in our lives. One of my greatest debts is owed to my first true mentor, Mrs. Kelly, who was my third-grade teacher at Coolidge Elementary School in Phoenix, Illinois, during the 1963–1964 school year. Coolidge School was a segregated enclave, nestled in a working-class African American community of laborers with traditional, old-school norms. Mrs. Kelly was African American, a great teacher and encourager who unleashed self-efficacy and unimaginable intellectual achievement in my life!

Mrs. Kelly always valued me as a person. I grew up in a poor, troubled family, but she made me feel as if I were the smartest person ever. You might say that I was a teacher's pet. In her class, I received all A grades. Consequently, she put me in charge of watching the entire class whenever she left (for brief moments). My job was to write down the names of the noisy or rowdy students who invariably acted up whenever she left. Of course, my grades on assignments, excellent class participation, and supervisory role did not endear me to the "gangbangers" in my class. Nevertheless, Mrs. Kelly affirmed everyone even in discipline.

During that year, many positive things happened to me under Mrs. Kelly's tutelage. She surreptitiously revealed to me that I was reading at a 12.9 level on the required SRA standardized tests. She permitted me to organize and develop her bulletin boards. From this assignment, I had to do research on the state of Hawaii, culminating in an essay that she loved! Consequently, Mrs. Kelly allowed me to read that script before the entire school as a third grader (Coolidge included kindergarten through eighth grade). She presented me as a prodigy, advocating for a "double promotion" due to my emerging academic prowess. From that time on, the entire school always treated me as if I were a Black genius all my years! I had enormous social capital because of the mentorship and sponsorship of Mrs. Kelly!

Fast-forward to sixth grade. Mrs. Kelly was a good friend with my sixth-grade teacher, Mrs. Crutchfield. Mrs. Crutchfield was in charge of organizing students for a prestigious gifted student program at Thornton High School in Harvey, Illinois. This program included all the schools, mostly White, for the entire district. Mrs. Kelly was my advocate, recommending me. However, my family was too poor to afford the modest tuition cost. To my surprise and benefit, Mrs. Crutchfield paid the sixty-seven dollars in tuition for me to attend. It was there that I blossomed tremendously in every intellectual task or competition. I was the head of the group, over more advantaged students from wealthier White schools. That experience taught me to look beyond racial myths or ideologies and rely always on God-given talents or intellectual abilities. Like the great African American pitcher Satchel Paige, from there I never looked back.

To this day, all my intellectual achievements have derived from Mrs. Kelly's tutelage and Mrs. Crutchfield's patronage. From them I learned not to worry about comparing myself to others, especially the dominant racial group. Rather, my task was to concentrate on learning and developing my God-given potential through tenacity, empathy, and hard work with dedication. They affirmed me meticulously, and the sweet aroma of their sacrifices or contributions was the atomic energy that has thrusted me to national and international heights. They inspired. They gave. Despite being at a segregated Black school until I reached eighth grade, my initial pathways have been key to how the Lord has ordered my steps through schooling and my subsequent career.

By judicial decree, Coolidge School was desegregated when I entered the eighth grade. My parents moved our family away from the area after my sophomore year at Thornridge High School in Dolton, Illinois. Years later, after I received my doctorate from the University of Chicago, I returned to find Mrs. Kelly and Mrs. Crutchfield to no avail. All information about them was lost. I was so very disappointed, but I recalled how I had joyfully thanked them so many times verbally and with cards during my elementary school days. What they did for me was invaluable, a legacy to cherish and pass on forever. They helped me overcome the vicissitudes of racism, inferiority, and complacency.

Proverbs 20:5 echoes in my life because of Mrs. Kelly and Mrs. Crutchfield. I cannot wait to greet them in heaven someday. Hallelujah to the Lord of Hosts (Psalm 37:23–24)!

29
WHAT'S THAT IN YOUR HAND?
Rev. Arthur Jackson

> *Moses answered, "What if they do not believe me or listen to me and say, 'The LORD did not appear to you'?" Then the LORD said to him, "What is that in your hand?"*
> EXODUS 4:1–2

Though the question "What is that in your hand?" (Exodus 4:2) was directed to Moses, it's one worth pondering by all who have been entrusted with gifts and resources from God to be used in the lives of others. And—that would be all of us!

Peter's writing in the first book that bears his name includes these words about gifts: "Each of you should use whatever gift you have received to serve others, as faithful stewards of God's grace in its various forms" (4:10). Two major categories of gifts follow next: speaking and serving. "If anyone speaks, they should do so as one who speaks the very words of God. If anyone serves, they should do so with the strength God provides" (v. 11).

My wife, Shirley, has core gifts of the serving variety, and for roughly ten years she mentored a young girl named Mercedes—faithfully exercising those gifts. Shirley's relationship with Mercedes started when she was a fifth grader at the school connected to the Christian social service agency where Shirley worked. The agency valued hands-on engagement with children and youth so much that they allowed employees like Shirley to spend time with their mentees during work hours.

What began as a work-related relationship blossomed and bore fruit far beyond the setting where it started. From Mercedes's years in grade school through high school and college, Shirley was present in her life. Meetups occasionally took place in our home, and it was not uncommon for Mercedes to leave our home with several kinds of baked goods. Special occasions in Mercedes's life were shared. Apple-picking trips and overnight stays with Shirley at a place available to our family would also include other members of Mercedes's family.

The fact that Shirley's relationship with Mercedes spanned generational lines reminds me of the "older women . . . younger women" language of Titus 2:3–5, where intergenerational relationships are encouraged:

> Likewise, teach the older women to be reverent in the way they live, not to be slanderers or addicted to much wine, but to teach what is good. Then they can urge the younger women to love their husbands and children, to be self-controlled and pure, to be busy at home, to be kind, and to be subject to their husbands, so that no one will malign the word of God.

From childhood to early adulthood, the investment was real, natural, and nurturing. Shirley was all in, heart and hands.

Sharing our lives significantly and consistently need not be complicated. The "What do I have to give?" question is a great place to start. What has God deposited in your life? People often start with self-deprecating statements like "I don't have . . ." or "I'm not like . . ." or "I didn't go to . . ." The reality is that you are "fearfully and wonderfully" and uniquely made (Psalm 139:14)! And who the Lord has made you and what He has entrusted to you are needed by someone.

The Lord's initial question to Moses in Exodus 4 was the beginning of an interesting dialogue. Even after the Lord manifested Himself to Moses (vv. 1–9), Moses still manifested symptoms of "I-can't-itis." "Moses said to the LORD, 'Pardon your servant, Lord.

I have never been eloquent, neither in the past nor since you have spoken to your servant. I am slow of speech and tongue'" (v. 10).

The Lord doesn't let us off the hook easily. His response to a reluctant Moses?

> The LORD said to him, "Who gave human beings their mouths? Who makes them deaf or mute? Who gives them sight or makes them blind? Is it not I, the LORD? Now go; I will help you speak and will teach you what to say." (vv. 11–12)

Finally, after realizing that he had met his match, Moses embarked on the mission.

What the Lord has put in your hand—He wants you to use it in His strength. Without fanfare, in faith, looking to the Lord, allow Him to use you—your hands, your voice, your influence—in the lives of others for His glory, their good, and your growth.

30
THE YANKEE WAY
Rev. Dr. Eric Moore

*Train up a child in the way he should go, even
when he grows older he will not abandon it.*
PROVERBS 22:6 NASB

When I was about ten years old, my dad became concerned about the young boys in our inner-city neighborhood. They seemed to have a lot of energy, but some of that energy was not being put to good use. So he decided to start a twelve-and-under baseball team. He named them the Detroit Yankees. His goal was to help expel this energy but at the same time teach the boys morals and help build good character. Of course, this applied to me as well.

Because I observed my dad up close and personal, I was able to see that my dad lived what he preached. However, the one thing that I never fully understood was, "Why do we always have to pray before every game?" All he would ever say to me is, "It's the Yankee Way."

The next year my dad convinced my uncle to start a fourteen-and-under team. That way the boys who had turned thirteen would have the opportunity to continue to play, along with being mentored. The following years he added eight-and-under, ten-and-under, sixteen-and-under, and eighteen-and-under teams. He built an entire organization for the purpose of helping to build character into these soon-to-be men. The organization became so large that at one time each age division had two teams. Besides being known as teams that played hard and fair, we were known for beginning every game with prayer.

By God's grace, my wife and I had a son. I wanted to expose him to the game that I loved playing when I was a kid. He joined a local team at the young age of eight. It was fun. My wife and I enjoyed cheering for him from the sidelines, but something seemed to be missing. What was missing? The emphasis on character.

Although we didn't live in the inner city, I asked my dad if his grandson could play for his organization. He said yes. The next thing I knew, I was the head coach of his team. My dad only asked one thing of me as a coach. He asked that I coach the "Yankee Way."

I coached my son until his high school years. Our teams played in recreational leagues, travel leagues, and travel tournaments. The goal was to play hard and fair and teach character. I can honestly say we started every game with prayer.

The last couple of years I felt the Lord wanted more than just prayer before the game. So we started inviting the opposing team to meet us at the pitcher's mound after the game to pray. Sometimes it would be one or two players or a coach. Sometimes the entire opposing team would pray with us. God used these moments to impact so many people in so many ways.

In one instance, a coach was so touched that he asked that his wife, who was battling cancer, could throw the first pitch of the game the next time we played. He offered to purchase all the refreshments so we could hang around after that next game and pray for his wife. We did, and it was the most beautiful occasion of a majority White team and a majority African American team eating pizza, gulping energy drinks, and having fun together. Oh, guess who was there? My dad.

It's the Yankee Way—the way of Jesus!

31

THE HANDS THAT SHAPED ME

Rev. Clifford S. Ice

I am reminded of your sincere faith,
which . . . now lives in you also.
2 TIMOTHY 1:5

Harry Edward Ice, Lee Andrew Spencer, Richard Berry, Charlie Speight, John W. Moore, T. Michael Flowers, Donovan Case, Curtis Jenkins, and Tony Warner. These are only some of the men who have helped to make and shape me.

My first mentor was my father, Harry Edward Ice. From his hand came the raw material that shaped me into the man I am today.

Some of my earliest memories are me watching him tie his necktie as he dressed for church, where he faithfully served as chairman of the deacon board. I also remember hearing him speaking of how God got his attention in the hospital, where he made a commitment to follow Christ. I can still see him going to work and then coming home at night by public transportation after working the afternoon shift in the factory. He didn't own a car until he was in his forties, but that did not stop him from getting awards at work for perfect attendance. He would also talk with me while soaking his tired feet, passing on wisdom that he felt I would need later as a man. Even though I did not appreciate or realize it at the time, that was what he was doing. One of his sayings was "You may fall in the mud in life, but you don't have to wallow in it. Get up, clean yourself off, and keep going."

I have more memories that I could include, but the ones most vivid to this day are his prayers, his reading of the Bible, his story of how God saved him, and his often-repeated desire to be able to say at the end of his life the words of Paul in 2 Timothy 4:7: "I have fought the good fight, I have finished the race, I have kept the faith." These memories of him provided some of the disciplines I needed to grow as a believer. I believe the Spirit of God working in his life exposed me to what I needed later after my own commitment to follow Christ. I saw him pray, heard his testimony, observed him reading and studying the Scriptures and giving me an example to follow of a committed life. I thank God for my first mentor, who was my father, and I got the chance to thank him for his love before he passed. Unfortunately, I never got the chance to tell him that I had come to know Jesus Christ, who he had come to know in that hospital room. I hope he knows now in glory.

My grandfather Lee Andrew Spencer remained faithful to Christ while living in a small town in Alabama under the ever-present shadow of racism and discrimination. Born in 1888 and dying in 1985, he experienced God's faithfulness in a world different than my own. Richard Berry, under whose ministry I was saved, always wanted to know how I was "really doing." Charlie Speight obeyed God and shared Christ with me before I could leave the room we were in. John W. Moore challenged me to step outside of my comfort zone and take a risk for the cause of Christ. Pastor T. Michael Flowers entrusted me with responsibility. Donovan Case took an interest in my welfare at a time when his experience, knowledge, and wisdom were what I needed to navigate through a turbulent and unsettling time in my life and ministry. My brother in Christ Curtis Jenkins came and took me with him as a companion as he ministered to the saints. And Tony Warner many times included me as a partner as he was faithfully persuaded about the ministry and the vision God gave him.

All these men have helped to shape me into who I am today. They all have been mentors to me at various seasons of my life. But it was my father who was the first mentor. Everything else was built on the foundation he laid.

Take the time to think about and thank the persons who—through the access they gave you into their lives and the sacrifice of time and energy given to you—have helped to make you who you are today.

32

"GRAB AHOLT AND HOLLER"

Dr. Michael R. Lyles

The LORD makes firm the steps of the one who delights in him; though he may stumble, he will not fall, for the LORD upholds him with his hand.

PSALM 37:23–24

My son grew up as a dedicated sports fan who dreamed of playing college football. In high school he played defensive safety on the football team. His coach was a loud, intense, in-your-face type of football "mentor" who was famous for yelling catchy phrases that sometimes had a deeper meaning.

At the end of his sophomore year, my son's team reached the state playoffs for his area's championship. They faced a team that featured a running back who would later go on to be a college All-American and a star in the National Football League. He was huge, fast, and ran with the attitude of a beast. My son was the third-string safety at the beginning of that game. The first-string safety was injured trying to tackle the "beast," who ran over him. The second-string safety saw the carnage of the first-string safety and began to scream that he had cramps. That left the third-string safety, my tenth-grade son, to face the "beast," who was taller, meaner, faster, and fifty pounds heavier.

The coach of my son's team was always one to be very direct with his "encouragement." He grabbed my son's face mask, stared intently into his eyes, and encouraged him in a thick Southern drawl. "You are too small and too slow to handle that big ole boy. That's why you have a team. So get in his way, grab aholt to something, and holler for help!" In other words, do what you can do, don't let go, and holler for help. True enough, he grabbed an arm, a leg, or a foot and held while yelling for help to arrive.

For many, team sports are a place where lessons in life are learned. Sometimes the lessons are taught by a mentor or coach. Sometimes they are learned in competition. At other times, they are modeled by peers. "Grab aholt and holler for help" was one of those lessons about recognizing one's limitations while also owning what one could and should do. Though a problem in life might be too big and intense to tackle alone, do your responsibility and ask, yell, or holler for help. If you holler for God (also known as *pray*), you may fall and feel like you will be trampled, but God will arrive to help before you are utterly cast down, as these verses in Psalm 37 so aptly promise.

Years later in college, my son would encounter a different kind of "beast" as he prepared to apply for law school. He was concerned about the challenge of gaining admission into his dream law schools. A part of him feared that he might not get into any quality law school. A part of him was tempted to "cramp up" in fear and not compete or try. However, he was reminded that he needed to do his part by grabbing "aholt" of his books and not letting go until he had given it his best effort. He learned that maturity was about learning how to "holler for help" from study groups and professors. He ultimately learned that life was not about avoiding getting run over by beasts—because everyone, no matter how good, will fall down under some burden.

The person in Psalm 37 was doing the right thing when life caused him to stumble and fall. However, he kept stepping forward and did not quit. We know this because he experienced being supported by the hand of God. That would not be the experience of someone rolling on the ground in defeat. Falling is just the beginning of the process. The real growth is in learning how to "grab aholt" of God, holler (pray), and experience the hand of God supporting you through those times.

Churches are like athletic teams where different people are gifted to play different positions. We are all going to be in positions where we are called to tackle a beast of a problem, relationship, or situation that we cannot handle alone. Life is not about running from an intimidating problem but instead doing what you can do and looking for help. Tackling that relationship challenge may be a process that involves being dragged painfully for a time. Tackling that situation may require a team effort—not just you. However, it does begin by grabbing what is our responsibility, not letting go, and hollering—until help arrives. That football coach taught a football lesson that turned into a life lesson that will last longer than the game . . . that they lost.

33

A WORD TO THE FATHERS

Dr. Ken Staley

Train up a child in the way he should go: and when he is old, he will not depart from it.

PROVERBS 22:6 KJV

Training is an action word. It is the process of teaching a person a particular skill or type of behavior. As a father, you are commanded by God to take the leadership role in raising your children . . . to point out to them the way toward loving the Lord with all their heart, mind, soul, and strength. To instill in them and stir up a desire to please the Lord in every area of their lives and to be transformed.

> Therefore, I urge you, brothers and sisters, in view of God's mercy, to offer your bodies as a living sacrifice, holy and pleasing to God—this is your true and proper worship. Do not conform to the pattern of this world, but be transformed by the renewing of your mind. Then you will be able to test and approve what God's will is—his good, pleasing and perfect will. (Romans 12:1–2)

Their standard for living and behavior is to be God's standard, not that of the world.

And what is "train[ing] up a child" if not mentoring? A father has a God-given responsibility and is accountable to God for mentoring, or training, his children. As a Christian parent you are to

> do your best to present yourself to God as one approved, a worker who does not need to be ashamed and who correctly handles the word of truth. (2 Timothy 2:15)

> And, ye fathers, provoke not your children to wrath: but bring them up in the nurture and admonition of the Lord. (Ephesians 6:4 KJV)

Nurture, according to Webster's *American Dictionary of the English Language*, is "that which promotes growth; education; instruction."* It includes everything that you do to guard your child's total spiritual and natural life . . . reading Scripture together and discussing the application of the passages, meeting your child's friends and their families to ensure they are not being exposed to dangerous influences, setting a strong example of living for Christ in word and deed. *Admonition*, according to Webster's dictionary, is "gentle reproof; counseling against a fault; instruction in duties; caution; direction."**

Sensitivity to the Holy Spirit and His leading is critical to being an effective father. Fathers should take the time to pray with and for each child (allowing the child to talk to God in their presence) so that daily prayer becomes a way of life for each. Understand that each child is an individual and has their own needs, place, and purpose in God's kingdom.

As a father, you are to cultivate a love for God, His Word, and His standard of living in your children. We fathers can only do that

---

* *American Dictionary of the English Language*, 1828 ed., s.v. "nurture," accessed April 27, 2023, https://webstersdictionary1828.com/Dictionary/nurture.

** *American Dictionary of the English Language*, 1828 ed., s.v. "admonition," accessed April 27, 2023, https://webstersdictionary1828.com/Dictionary/admonition.

if we come alongside our child and spend time together—not a few minutes in the morning or at night but spans of time—as we nurture, as we admonish, and as we mentor.

Your child's most important mentor is you.

34
A FATHER IS A MENTOR
Rev. Dr. Paul Cannings

*For I have chosen him, so that he will direct his children
and his household after him to keep the way of the LORD
by doing what is right and just, so that the LORD will
bring about for Abraham what he has promised him.*
GENESIS 18:19

A little boy followed his father as he carefully stepped through a new garden. He stepped exactly where his daddy stepped and said, "Daddy, if you don't get mud on your feet, I won't get any mud on me!" What a picture of the effect of a mentor! Just as God chose Abraham to direct his children, we as fathers have been chosen to lead our children.

We are extremely important to the development of the kingdom of God. God views us as His spiritual leaders in the home. It is our faithfulness to this task that qualifies us to serve in His house, the church: "If a man does not know how to manage his own household, how will he take care of the church of God?" (1 Timothy 3:5 NASB).

It is when a man chooses to be the spiritual leader in his home that God blesses his house and makes him prosperous (Proverbs 24:3–5; Psalm 128). For the salvation of our homes, our church, and our community, we must run this race that is set before us. "He will turn the hearts of the fathers back to their children and the hearts of the children to their fathers, so that I will not come and strike the land with complete destruction" (Malachi 4:6 NASB).

Being a leader and a mentor is sometimes very lonely. Many times, not even our wives understand or appreciate our vision for the home, our discipline of the children, or some of the decisions we make. However, we cannot back away from the role God has ordained for us. We cannot simply work for peace because, as spiritual leaders, all we will create is temporal peace as opposed to spiritual maturity. That maturity leads to peace that is more stable, and exhibits the Holy Spirit's fruit of love, joy, peace, patience, kindness, goodness, faithfulness, gentleness, and self-control (Galatians 5:22–23 NASB). Some of us may find that hard to accept. This is why a church men's ministry provides a place where men can come and share and be mentored and strengthened. "If we can share the load, we can bear the load" (see Galatians 6:2; 1 Thessalonians 5:14).

As we mentor our families, we need our wives to pray for us. Wives have words of wisdom, but trying to convince husbands through other means will never fix us the way prayer can, because when God does the fixing, He allows us to be the spiritual fathers we need to be, showing Himself strong as our spiritual Father. Watching a mate struggle through growth in our mentoring role within the family is helped by this prayer:

> For this reason I bend my knees before the Father, from whom every family in heaven and on earth derives its name, that He would grant you, according to the riches of His glory, to be strengthened with power through His Spirit in the inner self, so that Christ may dwell in your hearts through faith; and that you, being rooted and grounded in love, may be able to comprehend with all the saints what is the width and length and height and depth, and to know the love of Christ which surpasses knowledge, that you may be filled to all the fullness of God. (Ephesians 3:14–19)

35

WHEN WE SEE GOD
Rev. Dr. Henry Wells III

*In the year that King Uzziah died, I saw the Lord, high
and exalted, seated on a throne; and the train of his robe
filled the temple. Above him were seraphim, each with six
wings: With two wings they covered their faces, with two
they covered their feet, and with two they were flying. And
they were calling to one another: "Holy, holy, holy is the
L*ORD *Almighty; the whole earth is full of his glory." At the
sound of their voices the doorposts and thresholds shook and
the temple was filled with smoke. "Woe to me!" I cried.
"I am ruined! For I am a man of unclean lips, and I live
among a people of unclean lips, and my eyes have seen the
King, the L*ORD *Almighty." Then one of the seraphim flew
to me with a live coal in his hand, which he had taken
with tongs from the altar. With it he touched my mouth
and said, "See, this has touched your lips; your guilt is
taken away and your sin atoned for." Then I heard the
voice of the Lord saying, "Whom shall I send? And who
will go for us?" And I said, "Here am I. Send me!"*

ISAIAH 6:1–8

As a young Christian, much of what I saw and understood about God
was a result of my relationships with the men God placed in my life.
Unlike King Uzziah, and thankfully for me, the men in my life never
departed from the worship of the true God. I experienced God by
watching their success in marriage, in ministry, and in life.

Although King Uzziah was stricken with leprosy by the Lord for his disobedience, he did live the first part of his life as king of Israel worshipping God (2 Chronicles 26).

Uzziah had reigned for fifty-two years! His death signaled the end of a time of great prosperity and consistency. For the entire nation, it ushered in a time of uncertainty, change, and doubt. For Isaiah, Uzziah's death became the catalyst for him to have a personal encounter with God. He had seen Uzziah in his heyday as a faithful leader. He had also seen his downfall and demise. Now he would have to live without this example of faith and the consequences of disobedience.

There are seasons of life when the training wheels come off. These are times for deep self-reflection, greater awareness, and renewed commitment to our faith journey.

Apparently, Isaiah had his attention focused on Uzziah, but now that Uzziah was dead, his attention was redirected back to the Lord. Isaiah 6 depicts what the prophet saw when King Uzziah died. Isaiah saw God in His sovereignty, holiness, and glory. An earthly king may have died, but the Lord still reigned. He saw the Lord! We should anticipate and look forward to times in our lives when we see God more vividly and experience Him more profoundly.

Isaiah 6:5–7 depicts what the prophet sensed when King Uzziah died. No matter where we are on the Christian journey, there should always be a consciousness of our need for God. Continuous cleansing and renewal come from an awareness about our condition. "As it is written: 'There is no one righteous, not even one'" (Romans 3:10).

Thank God, the Lord does not just point out our sins; He also provides a means for our cleansing! With Isaiah, it was an angel with a live coal from the altar. With us, it is the precious blood of Jesus (1 John 1:7–9).

Isaiah did not stop at his cleansing. Sometimes we tend to get relief from God and stop there. God has so much more for us than just cleansing. If we say yes to God, it will open the door to life's purpose, fulfillment, and the joy that comes from serving God. In Isaiah 6:8,

Isaiah says, "Here am I. Send me!" Essentially, the prophet told God that he was available and eager to obey God's call.

The only response to seeing God as God is to repent. Our repentance results in an available and agreeable heart.

Isaiah was signifying that he was over the death of Uzziah and that his life was on the altar of sacrifice for the glory of God (Romans 12:1–2)! This reminds me of a statement popularized by the great evangelist Dwight L. Moody, who heard it at a prayer meeting: "The world has yet to see what God can do with and for and through and in a man who is fully and wholly consecrated to Him."

Our mentors are important, but they are no substitute for God Almighty! Isaiah found that out the hard way when the king that he so admired died. Certainly our mentors are important, but our commitment to submit, surrender, and sacrifice must be done with God first in our view.

36
DISCIPLES AS FRIENDS
Rev. Terry Robinson

Every day they continued to meet together in the temple courts. They broke bread in their homes and ate together with glad and sincere hearts.
ACTS 2:46

I no longer call you servants, because a servant does not know his master's business. Instead, I have called you friends, for everything that I learned from my Father I have made known to you.
JOHN 15:15

The phone rang at my mother-in-law's house, and the voice over the phone asked if Terry or Janice was present. The voice over the phone was Dr. Frederick G. Sampson's personal secretary. Dr. Sampson was a legendary Detroit pastor of Tabernacle Missionary Baptist Church and was featured frequently in *Ebony* magazine's list of the top one hundred African American preachers in America.

My mother-in-law quickly handed the phone to me. The next statement was no surprise to my ears but always a joy to my soul. "Dr. Sampson would like to treat you and Janice to dinner tomorrow night. Are you available? Great, he will meet you at Carl's Chop House at 6 p.m."

This would become a regular occurrence with my pastor and father in the ministry over the next twenty years. Sometimes it would be one-on-two with him and my wife. Other times it was with the ministerial staff and their wives. Other times it would be a mixture of laymen and ministers. In each case it would be a delicious occasion of food, fellowship, and fun. But most important were the electrifying nuggets of wisdom we would receive from "Doc," as he was affectionately known. Dr. Sampson was often known for his oratorical skills as a preacher of the gospel, but he was just as—if not more—effective in cultivating a relational environment.

Jim Putman and Bill Krause, in *Real-Life Discipleship Training Manual*, assert that "relationships are what God uses to communicate His truth and help people grow. Without relationships, the journey of discipleship is boring and ineffective. It may be informative, but it won't be life-changing."*

Doc had an incredible gift of cultivating a relational environment among the overall congregation and the core of his leadership. Sharing a meal together was one of his main ingredients.

> Day by day continuing with one mind in the temple, and breaking bread from house to house, they were taking their meals together with gladness and sincerity of heart, praising God and having favor with all the people. And the Lord was adding to their number day by day those who were being saved. (Acts 2:46–47 NASB)

In the early growth of the church in the first century there was a strong relational environment as many were turning to faith in Christ. One of the primary means of fellowship was the sharing of meals together from house to house.

Jesus was big on food, too. When He called to Zacchaeus, a hated tax collector who stole from the people from whom he was mandated by Rome to collect tribute, He asked to spend a night at his house.

---

* Jim Putman et al, *Real-Life Discipleship Training Manual: Equipping Disciples Who Make Disciples* (Colorado Springs, CO: NavPress, 2014), 60.

It was over a meal in this relational environment that Zacchaeus announced with no shame in his game that he would repay the monies that he had stolen.

> Jesus entered Jericho and was passing through. A man was there by the name of Zacchaeus; he was a chief tax collector and was wealthy. He wanted to see who Jesus was, but because he was short he could not see over the crowd. So he ran ahead and climbed a sycamore-fig tree to see him, since Jesus was coming that way.
>
> When Jesus reached the spot, he looked up and said to him, "Zacchaeus, come down immediately. I must stay at your house today." So he came down at once and welcomed him gladly.
>
> All the people saw this and began to mutter, "He has gone to be the guest of a sinner."
>
> But Zacchaeus stood up and said to the Lord, "Look, Lord! Here and now I give half of my possessions to the poor, and if I have cheated anybody out of anything, I will pay back four times the amount."
>
> Jesus said to him, "Today salvation has come to this house, because this man, too, is a son of Abraham. For the Son of Man came to seek and to save the lost." (Luke 19:1–10)

After coming to faith in Christ, Zacchaeus was convicted to turn from what he had been doing and make restitution. And it started with the simple act of eating together with Jesus.

I am grateful to my Lord and Savior for helping me see my spiritual mentor, Dr. Frederick G. Sampson, model this principle in an excellent way. I have sought to implement this in my discipleship ministry down through the years.

How are you doing in your disciple making? Is it heavy on information but light on life-on-life relationships? Why not start with a meal?

I think I said something!*

---

* "I think I said something!" was Dr. Sampson's signature phrase that he used after he said something profound, which was quite often.

37
LITTLE BROTHER: FROM CRACK TO PASTOR
Rev. Joseph Williams

And the things you have heard me say in the presence of many witnesses entrust to reliable people who will also be qualified to teach others.
2 TIMOTHY 2:2

Only five years prior to meeting Henry, I had struggled mightily with an addiction to heroin. The bulk of my income came from illegal activities, mostly selling drugs. I am so grateful that God miraculously brought me out of that miserable existence. God provided me with many opportunities to grow in my faith. I had become a minister and faithfully served my church. I was a student at a local Bible college. My professor Matthew Parker had become not only my teacher but also a trusted mentor. My new bride, Sharon, and I had recently had our first child. We were even able to purchase a home for our family.

Years earlier, as a prisoner at Leavenworth, I had learned the trade of furniture upholstery. I worked in this trade after release. I enjoyed working with my hands to create something beautiful out of something that was worn-out, dirty, and damaged. That's what God had done in my life. I operated an upholstery business out of the basement of our home. My clientele was growing.

I needed someone to help me in the shop. A year earlier I had left a position at the Detroit Rescue Mission (DRM) where I worked as a counselor for two years, serving men who suffered from the same affliction God had delivered me from. It was very fulfilling. I knew I could find a willing young man there to help me in the shop. This person would also have the opportunity to learn the trade. We would spend work hours in my home-shop, giving me an opportunity to model Christian manhood before him.

I contacted my friend Rev. Al Bufkin, who was the director at DRM. Al told me he had just the right guy for me. A twenty-four-year-old Henry Wells showed up at my home early the next morning. By his appearance it was evident that the streets had taken their toll on him. But he appeared sincere and eager to work and learn. I learned that Henry, like myself, had grown up attending church but strayed from the faith as a youth. Both his parents were Christians.

Growing up in the inner city of Detroit had proven to be too much of a challenge for the young man. Young people his age were making tons of cash selling crack cocaine. That life appeared very glamorous and alluring to many young people. Henry was no exception. As a teenager he left the church and hit the streets hard. He became a dealer of this terrible drug and soon became a victim of it himself. To the great dismay of his loving parents, he swiftly descended from a bright young Christian youth to a neighborhood crackhead.

Out of desperation, his parents took him to DRM. They hoped that going through their Bible-based program would help restore him to his former self. He had resided at DRM for only a short while when he was sent to work with me. We worked together, broke bread together, prayed together, and studied together throughout the day. We shared many lively discussions about life, faith, and manhood. He spent time with my new wife and child. I got to know his family.

Henry worked with me for about one year. During that time, he went beyond being an employee and mentee. He became my little brother. It would become a lifelong relationship. It was amazing seeing him so quickly reconnect to the faith that was instilled in him as a youth. In a short while he went from neighborhood crackhead to a student at the same Bible college I attended. He became a minister at his church. He even went to work at DRM, where he preached hope to many other young men who had fallen victim to the cruel streets.

Henry recently earned his doctorate in ministry. Now Rev. Dr. Henry Wells III serves as the senior pastor at New Beginnings Fellowship Church. He leads a Christian school in Detroit. His passion is serving young people. He has been married to his wife, Deborah, for thirty years and has two grown children. My four now-grown children call him Uncle Henry. I call him little brother.

Don't be afraid to let your mentee into your life. It is, truly, the only way that they can follow you as you follow Christ (1 Corinthians 11:1).

38

LIVING THE TRUTH
Dr. Henry Allen

*For the L*ORD *is good; his mercy is everlasting; and*
his truth endureth to all generations.
PSALM 100:5 KJV

I never ever had to consciously memorize Psalm 100:5 because it was imprinted in my soul by Rev. Alan Sanders, pastor of Mount Zion Missionary Baptist Church on Eighth Avenue in Phoenix, Illinois. On July 13, 1967, Rev. Sanders led me to a saving faith in the Lord Jesus Christ during vacation Bible school. I had just turned twelve years old the week before. My penultimate debt is to Rev. Sanders, for he was God's agent to save me and my younger brother, who died unexpectedly a few years ago. How great indeed was this unsung hero to me!

Rev. Sanders grew up in rural Mississippi. At age twelve, he met the Lord in a dramatic conversion he always celebrated every time he preached from 1967–1971. He had only an eighth-grade education and migrated north in his teen years to work in the steel mills in Gary, Indiana. Rev. Sanders spoke of his calling to the gospel ministry during that era. He moved to a little house in Phoenix, just down the street from the church he built as the inaugural pastor.

When I was eight years old, I had a crush on the girl next door. She was two years older than me, but she invited me to go to church with her at Mount Zion. Of course, I was delighted by that invitation, trying to get next to her to win her affections! But things backfired immensely because, as I was a visitor, the ushers sat me in the first row below the pulpit and altar area. Then, Pastor Sanders preached the scariest message I had ever heard about sin, judgment, and hell. I left the church frightened, forgot about my escort, and vowed never to ever return to church.

Years later, when I was twelve, my mother had acute marital trouble, suffering abuse with my alcoholic-prone father. She took my brother and me to church with her at Mount Zion! Was I ever petrified! Again, the ushers sat me with them in the very first row. But this time Rev. Sanders spoke about John 3:16, as well as God's love. He emphasized how God wanted to save everybody who accepted His invitation by faith. Wow! Was I ever shocked at this same minister as he exuded love, care, compassion, and kindness. He talked to my mother after service and invited me and my younger brother to vacation Bible school. Mom mandated us to attend!

During vacation Bible school, Rev. Sanders played softball and other games with us. He generously gave us food and treats. I could not believe he was the same person I met years earlier who preached about the horrors of hell! On July 13, 1967, just before lunch, he invited everyone to place their faith in the Lord Jesus Christ. At first, I hesitated until a girl who was severely disabled accepted Christ. Seeing that miracle, I was convicted to tears. Thus, I surrendered my life to Christ, with my brother following behind me despite my discouraging him to come up. Pastor Sanders rebuked me for telling him to not follow me to the altar—saying that my brother might also accept Christ as his Savior and Lord. Years later, as my younger brother died before me, I wept bitterly because I might have foolishly dissuaded him from salvation. Oh, how I cherish the wisdom and invitation of Rev. Alan Sanders, my father in faith. My brother died as an itinerant gospel minister with his own radio broadcast! What a miracle.

Years later, as my family moved away, I realized how pivotal Rev. Sanders had been in my life. He urged us to join the youth choir. He invited us to Sunday school, regular Sunday services, afternoon services, BTU (Baptist Training Union), and evening services. Moreover, we attended occasional Friday evening services, choir practice, as well as other activities. Pastor Sanders allowed us to ride in his nice vehicle whenever we visited other churches in Illinois or Gary, Indiana. He loved and took care of me and my brother, keeping us away from destructive temptations, crowds, and the turmoil at home! He was the embodiment of this passage from the book of James:

> Who is wise and understanding among you? Let them show it by their good life, by deeds done in the humility that comes from wisdom. But if you harbor bitter envy and selfish ambition in your hearts, do not boast about it or deny the truth. Such "wisdom" does not come down from heaven but is earthly, unspiritual, demonic. For where you have envy and selfish ambition, there you find disorder and every evil practice.
>
> But the wisdom that comes from heaven is first of all pure; then peace-loving, considerate, submissive, full of mercy and good fruit, impartial and sincere. Peacemakers who sow in peace reap a harvest of righteousness. (3:13–18)

He was my hero indeed. One thing Rev. Sanders did consistently was to cite Psalm 100:5 all his days. He said it so many times that it found its way to my spirit, where it has nestled all of my days since. I have known His goodness and everlasting mercy, I have seen His truth trump every falsehood that tried to make its way through my consciousness, and I have committed that truth to the next generation: my precious children and the young people with whom I have interacted over the years as a professor, teacher, and mentor.

I visited Rev. Sanders after receiving my doctorate. My employment journey led me to Minnesota, where I received the sad news of his death years later. Immediately, Psalm 100:5 exploded in my spirit!

I carry the legacy of Rev. Alan Sanders in all my endeavors. I am his disciple in Christ, the very highest honor in my life. He taught

39

SPEAK, LORD
Rev. Marvin Williams

So Eli told Samuel, "Go and lie down, and if he calls you,
say, 'Speak, LORD, for your servant is listening.'"
1 SAMUEL 3:9

"Dad, how do you know when and if God is speaking to you, and how can you distinguish God's voice from your own and Satan's?" my sixteen-year-old son asked me.

"Son, based on the examples in the Bible, God speaks to us through Scripture, the Holy Spirit, godly people, and circumstances. Moreover, it's probably not something you would have thought of on your own. Why do you ask?" I queried.

"Well, while I was in the shower, I think I heard God tell me to start a Bible study for my classmates."

I told him that what he heard sounded like something God would say and that he should obey. He admitted he didn't know the first thing about starting a Bible study and asked me if I would help him. I agreed.

For the next two weeks, he planned and strategized and asked me for feedback. I didn't tell him what to do, but I asked him questions and fielded his questions so he could spend time with the Lord discovering the answers for himself. If he was going to be resilient in the face of difficulty, it would be because he owned the vision God had given him for the Bible study.

To reach the most students and to achieve critical mass, we

thought it would be a good idea to have the Bible study at the school. So, he asked for a room and a teacher to sponsor the study, but neither was available. He was discouraged, but I reminded him that many times perceived obstacles are God's way of stretching our faith. With the school option off the table, he asked my wife and me if he could have the study at our house on Saturday evenings. We reluctantly agreed, though we didn't think our house and Saturday evenings were optimal choices. We learned profound lessons early in this process: God's ways are higher than our ways, and we needed to trust God to lead our son. As it turned out, our house was the perfect venue and Saturday was the best day for the Bible study.

The first week of the Bible study, he distributed flyers, inviting his classmates to the Bible study. The day arrived, and our entire family cleaned and prepared to welcome a throng of high school students into our home. Marvin Jr.'s faith would become sight, right? Not quite! Five people attended—me and his younger brother (he needed critical mass initially) and two classmates. That Marvin Jr. was discouraged, confused, and hurt was an understatement. "Dad, I thought God wanted me to start a Bible study. Where is the fruit of the God-given vision?" The initial results made him think that he hadn't really heard from God, and he wanted to quit. I wanted to assume the role of savior and deliver him from his despondency, but then he would miss all kinds of lessons and the opportunity to trust God. Like any good mentor, I encouraged him, prayed with him, and pointed him to his only Savior and Source—Jesus.

Marvin Jr. didn't quit but planned the second week. This time, eight people attended. The following week, twelve people attended. Slow growth is still growth. By the end of the school year, the Bible study averaged sixteen students. He ran the Bible study for two more years, averaging thirty-five students each week—all student led.

Like Eli mentored Samuel to respond to the Lord, I encouraged Marvin Jr. to listen to God and obey His promptings. The result of his obedience was kingdom impact. Many students surrendered their lives to Christ, are serving in various ministries throughout the country, and have begun discipling others. Also, God used Marvin Jr.'s obedience to fulfill a prayer that my wife and I had prayed before we moved to Lansing, Michigan: *Lord, use our home as a spiritual oasis in the desert and an incubator for discipleship and kingdom community.*

God called Marvin Jr., and he answered, "Here I am. Speak, Lord, your servant is listening." Because he listened and obeyed, God rewarded him with good fruit.

40
MULTIPLICATION THROUGH MENTORING
Rev. Reginald M. Holiday

Moses' father-in-law replied, "What you are doing is not good. You and these people who come to you will only wear yourselves out. The work is too heavy for you; you cannot handle it alone. Listen now to me and I will give you some advice, and may God be with you. You must be the people's representative before God and bring their disputes to him. Teach them his decrees and instructions, and show them the way they are to live and how they are to behave. But select capable men from all the people— men who fear God, trustworthy men who hate dishonest gain—and appoint them as officials over thousands, hundreds, fifties and tens. Have them serve as judges for the people at all times, but have them bring every difficult case to you; the simple cases they can decide themselves. That will make your load lighter, because they will share it with you. If you do this and God so commands, you will be able to stand the strain, and all these people will go home satisfied."
EXODUS 18:17–23

My maternal grandfather, Edward Hill, once saw me attempting to use a hammer. He told me, "Son, you're going to work yourself to death!" He took the hammer and showed me how to swing it properly, explaining it as he did. He then gave the hammer back to me and said, "There, you do it now." And lo and behold, following his example and learning from his experience, I not only drove the nail into the piece of wood but did so with one blow! He encouraged me and said, "Sometimes you have to work hard. But work smart every chance you can."

Quality mentors help us multiply our effectiveness. Take the case of Moses, the lawgiver in Exodus 18. Moses's father-in-law, Jethro, comes upon him toiling at his work, frustrated by its demands and overwhelmed by seeking to lead alone. Jethro assesses the situation, converses with Moses, and gives him very valuable advice. He instructs Moses that the way he is currently carrying out his work would not only lead to his undoing but also tax the Lord's people. So Jethro gives him specific parameters for getting others involved and sharing the load of ministering to more than one million people.

We need mentors who can come alongside us and assess what we are endeavoring to do and then give us insight into doing it better or multiplying our effectiveness. I have been mentored by individuals who saw my work and intuitively knew I could not continue under that load and stress. And so they pulled me aside, as did Jethro with Moses, and gave me wise counsel for how to multiply my effectiveness. Like Jethro, they did not present their wisdom in such a way that appeared dogmatic or diminishing regarding my role. Instead, they shared their knowledge from their experience, which made me more receptive as a mentee to what they were sharing.

Like Moses with Jethro, I had to take my grandfather's advice to garner better results. As Moses regarded Jethro's counsel, things improved for everyone.

> Moses listened to his father-in-law and did everything he said. He chose capable men from all Israel and made them leaders of the people, officials over thousands, hundreds, fifties and tens. They served as judges for the people at all times. The difficult cases

they brought to Moses, but the simple ones they decided themselves. (Exodus 18:24–26)

As Moses followed Jethro's advice, he not only got the job done more effectively but also allowed other capable leaders to contribute and share the burden. Someone once said, "If you want to go fast, go by yourself. If you want to go far, go with others." Mentees can go further than they might be able to otherwise with the right advice from a mentor.

One of the tremendous benefits of being mentored by those who have learned from their own experiences is not necessarily having to repeat their errors or struggles. Contrary to popular belief, experience is not the best teacher. *Applied* experience is the best teacher. We all should be grateful for those who will share with us the benefit of their perspective to help us become more effective at what we do.

Want to go from good to great? Avail yourself of mentors who will help you multiply, amplify, and extend what you are already doing!

DESIGN TO BUILD
BLACK MEN*
Colin Pinkney

*And they said, "Let us rise up and build." So they
strengthened their hands for this good work.*
NEHEMIAH 2:18 KJV

There is a portrait of Julian Francis Abele that hangs in the administrative office building of Duke University in Durham, North Carolina. Abele is the architect credited with designing many of the ornate
buildings on the campus of Duke. As well, he planned the site layout
of the campus. Young Julian Abele was educated at the Institute for
Colored Youth, Brown Prep School, and the Philadelphia Museum
School of Industrial Art before enrolling at the University of Penn-
sylvania in 1898. An outstanding student, Abele received a number
of prizes during his undergraduate years at Penn. After graduating in
1902 with his degree in architecture, Abele was immediately engaged
by established architect Horace Trumbauer—who helped to finance
the young architect's three years of study in Paris!

Abele became responsible for the design of such Philadelphia
buildings as the Philadelphia Museum of Art, the Free Library of
Philadelphia, the Land Title Building, and a number of mansions.

Abele's projects outside Philadelphia include the Widener Memorial Library in Cambridge, Massachusetts, mansions in Newport and in New York, and many of the English Gothic and Georgian buildings on the campus of Duke University.

As a young boy I was always fascinated with architecture and drawings of buildings and houses, and I believed architects were really important people. A two-year stint of drafting classes in high school was the extent of my pursuit of a professional life as an architect. But the notion of design never left me. I believed I could become a great architect as I satiated my fix for design, peering over the shoulder of my older brother Bill as he painted portraits and designed blueprints. He also had a special talent for bringing an intimate look at the lives of Black folks to his paintings. We all admired Bill for his talent. I was and still am most fascinated by his ability to draw and sketch structures; he could take the back of a napkin and draw something on the order of the Eiffel Tower in a matter of minutes.

While I was a student at North Carolina State University I lived with Bill and his family, and I always looked forward to the opportunity to visit his office in Chapel Hill where he worked as an architect apprentice. He would often pull out a blueprint of some building or grand structure that he was working on and explain to me all of the intricate details of every shape and measurement. Bill is a gifted technician of design and an accomplished fine artist. In fact, the artist's name at the bottom of the Abele portrait is his: William Alton Pinkney III.

Although I did not grow up to design buildings or structures like Abele or my brother Bill, I have become an architect of sorts. I grew up without my father, like most Black men I know. My God-given passion is to restore a stable and biblical value of marriage and family in the heart of every young Black male. My role has been to help design wraparound services to serve families coming out of homelessness, and to serve boys in programs that help build their lives.

I believe that if we start with a clear and relevant definition for manhood, our community will gain a new value for young African

American boys and what they can become in their journey into manhood.

The young men I mentor have recognized that materialistic-based values are short-lived and do not offer them the life they truly seek to build. I am always amazed in the "We Are World Class" book club that we have designed when I ask the young men about marriage. It never fails that 100 percent of the young men raise their hands when I inquire about their desire to be married and have families.

I believe it's time we had a laymen's discussion about how each of us can take part in shaping future Black families as we help mold young Black men. As an African American man raising African American sons, I have a responsibility to offer them a working blueprint that will mold them into competent men of high value and character. When all is said and done our children should be a resource to the community.

Not having my father in my life after the age of eight forced me to search for external guidance into manhood. Many of my missteps and failures have led me down a path of research and discovery that has shaped who I am and fueled my passion to help as many other young Black men as I can. I'm convinced that every adult in our community has a stake in this endeavor. We have the power and the access to reconstruct our homes and communities.

If our sons are to fulfill their God-given destinies, we must make them understand and translate for them the things that matter most. As parents, guardians, and mentors, we must become fully engaged in the reality that nothing our sons experience in life is without consequence. Every little thing matters; when it comes to raising our sons and mentoring at-risk young men, we cannot take anything for granted.

What does it mean to be a man? What is expected of a man by his family, society, and peer group? These are valid and perplexing questions for boys living in our society with the definitions for many of our social norms having been called into question due to a lack of tradition and what I call *social triumphs*. I consider social triumphs to be healthy and stable two-parent-led households, supportive community services that emphasize empowerment over enablement, and solid academic centers at the primary, secondary, and postsecondary levels that strengthen the minds of young men, offering them a strong moral compass for a living. Our churches should be at the forefront of these social structures. In an ideal world, churches and communities of faith operate as the center of moral guidance for a young man.

Imagine how different things would be if a large majority of our families and communities agreed on an inspired and value-based definition for manhood. Not only would we raise our sons differently; we would also have much clearer and higher expectations for them and what they could become. Can you imagine what kind of community that would be? Our teachers would engage little boys differently and be sure not to demotivate them with culturally biased and gender-biased teaching methods. Our coaches would be more careful on the game field to model a kind of competitiveness that is truly team-oriented and that de-emphasizes selfish attitudes. Our religious leaders would be more careful not to use their spiritual authority to violate boys emotionally and sexually. Ultimately, parents would be intentional in teaching their sons the value of work and the dignity of being adequate providers for their families. I believe our prisons would become ghost towns and the crowded hallways of social service agencies would be empty.

Being a man is more than a matter of biology. After my own journey and quite a bit of study and research, I've concluded that the following definition of manhood offers the best framework and vision for young Black males to live productive lives: a man is one who seeks to live a godly lifestyle, models healthy living, and provides a positive impact on others in his family and community. Even with this clear definition, I believe the bigger question is: When does it start?

I believe there are four basic activities of manhood that we should teach and instill in boys as early as third grade:

A man leads with courage. He's out front on the important issues and willing to be responsible for the results in his life, family, and community.

A man serves with humility. He rejects machismo and pride, and he gives his time, talents, and resources to influence the world for good.

A man loves unconditionally. The big lie of previous generations is that men are intrinsically unemotional and detached. We have accepted the notion that nurturing and care are primarily female-oriented traits. Nothing could be further from the truth. Emotional caring is gender-neutral. Unconditional love is passionate, thoughtful, and grace-filled, and it is essential for men to provide this in their relationships with their children.

If we raise our sons to be more expressive of their feelings, we improve outcomes for future marriages, families, and communities. One of the best opportunities we have to grow sons who love unconditionally is to teach them the value of forgiveness, particularly where a father has failed to model manhood principles.

A man provides consistently for his family.

The good news is that though these traits may seem archaic and unattainable, they are very relevant and possible to achieve for every young man. These principles have informed the mentoring work that I do. Sadly, these attributes are in direct opposition to most of the imagery and expectations set forth in the hearts and minds of young Black males. To gain traction in this important transition, it will be necessary to deconstruct the false and harmful modern-day notions of manhood and leadership.

Before we try to impact the overt realities of self-image and social behavior distortions, we must translate for our sons the core elements for living a healthy and successful life. I believe we can save our sons. I believe they can achieve and live up to their highest potential. Most important, I believe that group mentoring is a vital key to help our sons do that. "Do nothing out of selfish ambition or vain conceit. Rather, in humility value others above yourselves, not looking to your own interests but each of you to the interests of the others" (Philippians 2:3–4).

When I think about a great mentor, I think of authentic men who care for their mentees in the same manner that a great father cares for his children. Great mentors are wholehearted men who are willing to share their secret of success with others. The key is that they share from a position of humility and authenticity. I have found that boastful and arrogant men do not make great mentors.

I find that mentors who have not dealt with the emotional pain inflicted on them by their dads struggle to offer authentic and loving relationships to the young men in their lives. It is a strange thing to witness unhealthy men ask young men to take their unhealthy examples and build something productive from those examples, all under the pretext of mentoring. I'm here to say that it will not work because it has not worked.

The vast majority of the young Black men in our country continue to live far below their academic, social, and career potential. To continue to point our collective finger at the failures in the educational, governmental, and social arenas is shortsighted. Men who want to make the most difference in the lives of young men should look in the mirror and make the changes needed to be great mentors. The foundation of great mentoring is for mentors to be emotionally and spiritually healthy. That will take some time and will require a series of training, development, and coaching. Mentors will only produce what they are, and we must take the time to develop great mentors so they can produce great results in the lives of young Black males. This must be the purpose of our mentoring.

Men, let us arise and build!

Colin Pinkney, Chaplain
NBA Charlotte Hornets

ACKNOWLEDGMENTS

I want to thank the Black men who poured out of the deepest parts of their hearts to put pen to paper, or finger to keystroke, to write these honest words of encouragement and transparency. Contrary to popular belief, we are neither dangerous nor expendable. We are human beings who are loved by an all-powerful, all-knowing God. We are, every day, straining to find our way in the world . . . and looking for people who already know that Way. I appreciate you all.

To the reader: Resist the temptation to give up on yourself because God never does. And we won't either. The authors you read between these book covers are praying men, and you can rest assured that they are already praying for you, whom they may not know, to the One who knows all. You are never alone in God's kingdom.

Matthew Parker

CONTRIBUTORS

Henry Lee "Hank" Allen, PhD, has been active as a sociologist, consultant, professor, and author for nearly four decades, serving as a professor at several colleges including Calvin University in Grand Rapids, Michigan, and Wheaton College in Wheaton, Illinois. He has published in numerous books and periodicals, focusing on violence in minority communities, police violence, violence against women, and the sociology of hate.

Karl Bell serves as managing director of GAA New Ventures, LLC, which focuses on economic and commercial real estate development in states throughout the Midwest and South. Formerly a senior vice president at Invest Detroit, which funds business expansion and real estate development, he has played a key role in Detroit's resurgence over the last decade.

Lloyd Blue, DMin, is chief executive officer of Church Growth Unlimited, headquartered in Mendenhall, Mississippi, and is the former pastor of North Oakland Missionary Baptist Church in Oakland, California. He is nationally acclaimed for his lectures in the areas of personal evangelism and discipleship, pastoral management and counseling, and expository preaching and revival.

Paul Cannings, PhD, serves as pastor of Living Word Fellowship Church in Houston, Texas; founder and president of Power Walk Ministries, a national and global training resource for clergy and lay leaders; president of Living Word Christian Academy; and adjunct professor at the College of Biblical Studies in Houston, Texas. He hosts daily and weekly radio programs.

Odell Cleveland is chief administrative officer of Mount Zion Baptist Church in Greensboro, North Carolina. He founded America's first faith-based community action agency, the Welfare Reform

Liaison Project, now a $100 million nonprofit organization with an outsized impact on North Carolina's most marginalized, and advises and guides public leaders based on his successes.

Reginald M. Holiday, pastor of Bethany Fellowship Church in Greensboro, North Carolina, is a grateful husband, father, and grandfather. He is the author of *#LeadWell: A 31-Day Leadership Development Devotional* and serves as an international Christian leader and equipper.

Noel Hutchinson, DMin, is the pastor of Kingdom Fellowship Baptist Church in Memphis, Tennessee, the executive mission director for the Progressive National Baptist Convention, and an adjunct professor at Memphis Theological Seminary and the Tennessee School of Religion. He is also the author of *From the Shepherd's Staff: The Remix* and has contributed several devotions to Our Daily Bread VOICES.

Clifford S. Ice, DD, serves as senior pastor of Community Bible Chapel and vice president and provost of Carver College, both in Atlanta, Georgia; founder and president of HOPE Ministries; and board member of the Southern Gospel Mission Association and Stewards Ministries. He and his wife, Lee Margarite Ice, have two daughters and two grandsons.

Arthur Jackson returned to Kansas City in 2016 after serving on pastoral teams at three churches in the Chicago area. He now serves as the Midwest region assistant director for PastorServe, a ministry that helps pastors and churches to be healthy. He and his wife, Shirley, have been married for fifty-four years.

Lee N. June, PhD, is a professor in the Honors College and Department of Psychology at Michigan State University. He also serves on the ministerial staff and teaches Sunday school at New Mount Calvary Baptist Church in Lansing, Michigan.

Michael R. Lyles, MD, is a nationally renowned psychiatrist in private practice who has served as assistant professor of psychiatry at the University of Kentucky. He has presented to more than thirty thousand physicians, mental health professionals, and lay counselors, and serves on the boards of several faith-based organizations that seek to reduce the stigma around mental health and increase access to mental health services.

James "Jimmy" McGee III is president and CEO of The Impact Movement based in Atlanta, Georgia. Impact is a national campus ministry serving Black students on various campuses throughout the United States. A native Chicagoan, he is a husband and father of three sons.

Eric W. Moore, DMin, is professor and chair of applied theology at Moody Theological Seminary. He is the author of *Pastoring the Small Church* (Resource Publications, 2013) and a contributor to the *One Volume Seminary* (Moody Publishers, 2022). In addition he is the pastor and cofounder of Tree of Life Bible Fellowship Church in Royal Oak, Michigan.

Matthew Parker, DD, is the founder of The Global Summit, a consortium of African American Christian churches and ministries, and of the Institute for Black Family Development, which strengthens the local community by providing training, technical assistance, and resources to serve children, youth, and families. He has had numerous partnerships with Christian publishers and is a noted consultant to public and private institutions including the state of Michigan, The Skillman Foundation (Michigan), Mendenhall Ministries (Mississippi), and Convoy of Hope (Missouri).

Colin Pinkney, executive director of the Harvest Center, a faith-based organization that serves the homeless, is a seasoned, award-winning community leader and change architect. He is a champion of healthy models for fathering, manhood, and leadership, and has mentored and trained more than six thousand men in various venues.

Terry Robinson and his wife, Janice, have been on staff with Cru, a national campus ministry, for forty-three years, including forty in Detroit, Michigan. He also serves as associate minister at Tabernacle Missionary Baptist Church in Detroit and on the advisory board for Moody Theological Seminary–Michigan.

Ken Staley, DMin, president of the Philadelphia Center of Urban Theological Studies, sits on numerous boards including the Philadelphia Prison Board, Geneva College, Lancaster Bible College, Christian Research & Development, and Mendenhall Ministries. He is also a certified clinical marriage and family therapist and serves as a chaplain with the Philadelphia Police Department.

Henry Wells III serves as the executive director of Westside Christian Academy and the senior pastor of New Beginnings Fellowship Church. His professional experience expands over thirty-four years of working in church-based and faith-based nonprofit organizations. Henry and his wife of thirty-three years are the proud parents of two children, Robert J. Wells and Melanie Elizabeth Wells.

Michael T. Westbrook, a US urban missionary, has served youth, teens, and families as cofounder, president, and CEO of Greater Life, Inc. since 1986 and as cofounder and pastor of Greater Life Christian Fellowship Church since 1998, both in the city of Newark, New Jersey. He is the president of The Global Summit, an African American leadership development group, since 2018.

Joseph Williams serves as cofounder of The Nehemiah Consortium, which seeks to restore the lives of those affected by crime and counts among its clients the US Department of Justice, the Billy Graham Center, the Southern Baptist Convention, and the Annie E. Casey Foundation. He is known for his innovative approaches to restoring prisoners and ex-offenders.

Marvin Williams serves as lead pastor of Trinity Church in Lansing, Michigan, and was one of the lead architects of Tabernacle Community Church in Grand Rapids, Michigan. He is an author and speaker for Our Daily Bread Ministries. He blogs about culture, diversity, Jesus, life, leadership, and spiritual formation.

C. Jeffrey Wright, JD, is president and chief executive officer of UMI (Urban Ministries, Inc.), a Christian media and publishing firm that has served African American churches with curriculum and other Bible study resources for more than fifty years. He came to UMI from a career in finance with two *Fortune* 50 companies. He is also a licensed minister.

General Editors

Joyce Dinkins loves collaborations that encourage successful publishing. She was an originator of David C. Cook's *Echoes*, helped grow NavPress magazines, and managed New Hope Publishers' growth. As an Our Daily Bread Ministries executive editor, she helped launch VOICES. Joyce directs Publishing in Color and creates through Joyce Dinkins Publishing LLC.

Diane Proctor Reeder writes primarily on spiritual topics that move readers to think more deeply about their faith and lives. She is an editor, playwright, and business owner of Written Images. Diane has served as an editor for Urban Ministries, Inc., Parker Books, and Our Daily Bread Publishing's Voices Collection.

Spread the Word
by Doing One Thing.

- Give a copy of this book as a gift.

- Share the QR code link via your social media.

- Write a review of this book on your blog, favorite
  bookseller's website, or at ODB.org/store.

- Recommend this book to your church, small
  group, or book club.

Connect with us. [f] [⦿] [𝕐]

Our Daily Bread Publishing
PO Box 3566, Grand Rapids, MI 49501, USA
Email: books@odb.org

Children's books from the Voices Collection

<<

Shout for Joy!

Children will learn to trust God and sing His praises in this paraphrase of Psalm 100 featuring captivating illustration from **Jan Spivey Gilchrist**.

>>

A Voice as Soft as a Honey Bee's Flutter

Journey with Junior as he learns to listen for the voice of God. Young readers and their grown-ups experience the wisdom of Psalm 46 through a colorful masterpiece by award-winning author and illustrator **Jan Spivey Gilchrist**.

<<

You See Me, God

Children learn that their heavenly Father loves them and created them with a purpose.

OTHER TITLES IN THE VOICES COLLECTION

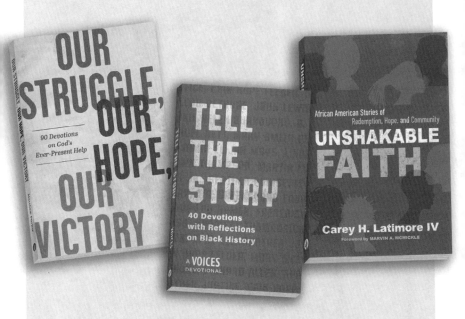

Available at

*https://ourdailybreadpublishing.org/voicescollection.html,
Amazon, or your local bookstore*